9/3

2⁰⁰

THE BOY I LEFT

BEHIND ME

THE BOY I LEFT

BEHIND ME

by

Stephen Leacock

DOUBLEDAY & COMPANY, INC.

Garden City   1946   New York

PUBLISHER'S NOTE

AT THE TIME OF HIS DEATH IN March 1944 Stephen Leacock had completed four chapters of memoirs which were to have been the beginning of his autobiography. It is a distinct loss that the full, rounded autobiography can never be written, but as Dr. Leacock's own record of his early years from childhood to young manhood these few chapters are a completely unified and delightful whole. It was his own idea to call the autobiography "My Memories and What I Think," and the title would be as truly descriptive of the little book presented here. However, as it has perforce been narrowed to his youth, in the long look back from his seventies, we think he would have liked our title, The Boy I Left Behind Me.

CONTENTS

THERE WILL ALWAYS

BE AN ENGLAND

I WAS BORN in Victorian England on December thirtieth in 1869, which is exactly the middle year of Queen Victoria's reign. If I were analyzed by one of those scientific French biographers who take full account of the time, the place, the circumstance, or by the new school of psychologists who study "behaviour," I imagine much could be made of this. As expressed in a plain sense, I am certain that I have never got over it.

I was born at Swanmore, which is a hamlet and parish on "Waltham Chase" in Hampshire. They use names like that in Hampshire because it is so old; it doesn't say who chased who: they may have forgotten. Anyway, it is a mile and a half from Bishop's Waltham, which is ten miles from Winchester and of which details may be had by consulting Domesday Book, though of course there is earlier information also. One reason why one feels proud of being born in Hampshire is that it is all of such immemorial antiquity. The Norman Conquest there is just nothing. Porchester and Winchester and Chichester are all a thousand years older than that.

I fell into an error about my birthplace and put it into print a good many times during the several years it lasted, so that I came near to having the honour of a disputed birthplace, like Homer and Mr. Irvin Cobb. It was Irvin Cobb, was it not, who said he had nearly got one but couldn't keep the dispute going? Mine arose quite innocently. I discovered that there is a Swanmore which is a suburb of Ryde in the Isle of Wight, and as I know that my grandfather lived near Ryde, I moved my birthplace into that suburb. Finding there was doubt, I wrote to a solicitor at Ryde who had conducted the family business of the Leacocks for generations and asked about it. He wrote that he thought it extremely unlikely that I was born in such a locality as Swanmore, Ryde. But I didn't know whether this was one on Swanmore or one on me, whether Swanmore was not fit for me to be born in or whether I had not the required class for Swan-more. So it stands at that. In any case it was in 1869, and Swanmore may have picked up since.

But I was led by this to write to the Vicar of Bishop's Waltham, and he sent me back a certifi-cate of my birth and christening at Swanmore Par-ish Church, and he said that not only was I born in Swanmore but that Hampshire was proud of it. This gave me such a warm thrill of affection for Hampshire that I very nearly renewed my sub-scription (one guinea per annum) to the Hamp-shire Society: very nearly—not quite. I knew they'd take the guinea, but I was not sure how they'd feel about it. People who come from celebrated places like Hampshire, known to all the world, and go away and don't see them again year after year, are apt to get warm rushes of sudden affection and pride towards the good old place. I've known peo-ple to feel this way towards Texas or Newfound-land or in fact anywhere to which you can't get back.

In such a glow of feeling years ago I subscribed to the Hampshire Society (one guinea per an-num), and it was certainly a delight at first to get

the annual circular, with the names of the Lord
Lieutenant and a lot of people as fellow members,
and the receipts and disbursements, and the balance carried forward—excitements like that. So it
went on that way year after year for years—a guinea
and a guinea and a guinea—till one year all of a
sudden I got an angry fit of economy (in the de-
pression) and asked, What am I getting out of all
this?—a guinea and a guinea—that could go on
forever—and I wrote and cut out my membership.
It's nothing against Hampshire. People do that t⌒
Texas and Newfoundland. And in any case it was
in the same year and about the same time that I cut
out my subscriptions to the Royal Society of Canada and the Authors' Association—even to things
that I didn't belong to. But it seemed a dirty trick
to have dropped the Hampshire Society and to
have fallen out of the Receipts and Disbursements and General Balance.

My family were Hampshire people on both sides
—not, of course, the real thing, going back to the

Conquest, but not bad. The Leacocks lived on the Isle of Wight, where my grandfather had a house called Oak Hill near Ryde, but I gather that he wanted the island for himself and didn't want his sons to come crowding onto it. That's why they were sent out across the world wherever it was farthest. The Leacocks had made a lot of money out of plantations in Madeira and the Madeira wine trade, so much that my great-grandfather John Leacock had retired and bought the house at Oak Hill. After that nobody in the family did any work (any real work) for three generations, after which, in my generation, we were all broke and had to start work—and work in the low-down sense, where you work by the hour, a thing that would disqualify anybody in Hampshire right off the bat. My brothers, I think, got seventeen cents an hour. I got a cent a minute, but that was as a schoolteacher. But I am anticipating and I turn back.

The Leacocks, I say, were in Madeira wine and the wine trade, and some of my cousins are still there and still in it. The senior member of the family got out a few years ago a booklet about Madeira wines and the Leacock family and he put

into it the fatal sentence: "The first recorded Leacock was a London day labourer, whose son was
brought up at a charity school and went out as a
ship's cabin boy to Madeira!" Think of it! What
can you do after that? It's no use going on to say
what a wonderful fellow the ship's cabin boy was
and how he built up great plantations and ownerships. That's no good. You can't get over that day-
labourer stuff. The Lord Lieutenant of Hampshire
knows just where to class me.

My mother's family, the Butlers, were much
better, though you couldn't really call them Hampshire people as they had not, at the time of which
I speak, been in Hampshire for more than one hundred and fifty years. They lived, and do still, in a
house called Bury Lodge, which is on a hill overlooking the immemorial village of Hambledon,
Hants, a village so old that they talk there of the
Great Plague of 1666, when so many people were
buried in the churchyard, as an affliction of yesterday. Hambledon, Hants, is to all people who play
cricket and love the game as Mecca is to a Mo-
hammedan. Here, more than anywhere else, began
the sacred game—for there is no other adjective

that can convey what cricket means to Englishmen
than the word "sacred." Here, on the wind-swept
open space of "Broadhalfpenny Down," was bowled
the first ball, the first rushing underhand ball where
bowling began. Here men in top hats planned and
named the game, designated, by a flight of daring
fancy, the strip of ground between the wickets as
the "pitch," indicated the right side of the batter as
the "on" side and the left as the "off" side—names
taken from the English carriage driving—christened
the brave man fielding thirty feet behind the batter's
bat as "square leg" (he needed to be), invented the
"over" and the "wide" and the "no ball" and
L.B.W.—to be carried round the world later as the
abiding bond of the British Empire.

The Butler family were intimately concerned
with the beginnings of cricket, and in the drawing
room of Bury Lodge are preserved (on blue foolscap
paper, gummed onto the fire screens) some of the
earliest scores at Broadhalfpenny Down. When I
was lecturing in London in 1921 I mentioned to
E. V. Lucas, the famous humorist (also one of the
great authorities on cricket) this family connection
and the old score sheets at Bury Lodge. I found/

that he at once regarded me with a sort of reverence. Nothing would do him but we must drive down to Hampshire to look at them. This we did, Lucas supplying the car, while I felt that my presence with him was compensation enough. The house was shut up, as the Butlers were in London, but a housekeeper showed us the scores, and then we drove up to Broadhalfpenny Down and stood there in the wind—well, just as people stand on the ruins of Carthage. After that we went down into Hambledon village and to the "pub," where I had all that peculiar gratification that goes with "the return of the native." There were several old men around, and it was astonishing what they could remember over a pint of beer, and still more over a quart. I had been away from Hambledon for nearly fifty years, so it enabled one to play the part of Rip van Winkle. I didn't mention that I had been there only once before, for ten minutes, as a child of six.

Generally the return of the native to his native town (for its old home week or for what not) is apt to be spoiled by the fact that after all he hasn't been away long enough, only ten or a dozen years at most. So when he says, "What's become of the queer old cuss who used to keep the drugstore? When did he die?" they answer in chorus, "He's not dead. He's right there still." In such circumstances never say that you'd give ten dollars to see so-and-so again, or they'll go and bring him.

As I say, my grandfather needed all the Isle of Wight to himself, and so when my father married my mother, whose name was Agnes Butler, daughter of the Reverend Stephen Butler, they were promptly sent out to South Africa. That was in 1866–67, long before the days of diamonds and gold created the South Africa of sorrows that came later. Those were the days of sailing ships, of infinite distances and of long farewells. They went "upcountry" to Maritzburg in oxcarts and then out beyond it to settle. It was all as primitive then as we see it in the movies that deal with Dr. Livingstone and darkest Africa. I saw Maritzburg forty years later, when its people seemed a mass of Asiatics, the immigrant wave from India that first awoke South Africa to the "Asiatic peril."

Maritzburg in 1867 no doubt appeared singularly quiet, but to those who lived there the whole place, as my mother has told me, was "seething with the Colenso controversy." I imagine few people of to-day remember the name of Colenso, the Bishop of Natal, the mathematician over whose *Arithmetic* and *Algebra* a generation of English schoolboys groaned and whose mild aspersions on the Penta-teuch—I think it means the first five books of the Old Testament—opened the way, like a water leak in a dam, to heresies that swept away the literal interpretation of Scripture. Colenso became a sort of test case, in orthodoxy, and in the law as to the government of the Church of England in the colo-nies, and locally a test case in the fidelity of the con-gregation. Some people in Natal would allow their children to be baptised by the bishop and some wouldn't and held them over for the dean any time the bishop was away. My eldest brother, who was born in Natal, got caught up in this controversy and was torn backward and forward before he could be christened. But the South African climate proved impossible for my mother and the locusts ate up their farm, and so the family came home again to Hampshire.

My grandfather then took another big think as to where he would send them to, and it was in this interregnum of thinking that my father was supposed to be "learning farming" to fit him to be sent to America. There was at that time in England a prevalent myth that farming could be "learned," especially by young men who couldn't learn anything else. So my father seems to have been moved round from one centre to another, drinking beer under the tutelage of Hampshire farmers—who, of course, could drink more than he could—an agreeable life in which a young man was supposed to remain a gentleman even if he acted like a farmer. As those of us who have been brought up on farms know, you can't "learn farming," at least not that way. We could, in fact, whisper to one another the way you learn it. First of all, as Course No. 1, First Year Agronomics, you get onto a wagonload of manure at six in the morning and drive up and down a seven-acre field throwing it in all directions, in fact seeing how far you can throw it. Then you go back for another load. Course No. 2, or Cultivation, involves driving two horses hitched to what is called a set of field harrow up and down a dry ploughed field so as to turn it into a cloud of dust and thistledown. During the driving you shout *Gee* and *Haw* at the horses. They don't know what it means, but they are used to hearing it and they know where to go anyway. Courses like that, carried on systematically over a period of years, make a man a farmer.

Of course I don't deny that over this and above it are the real courses in agriculture such as they teach at Ste. Anne's, P.Q., out near Montreal, and at the Ontario Agricultural College at Guelph, both splendid places. Here a student goes at it all scientifically, learning the chemistry of the thing and the composition of soils and all that. Hence when he goes back onto the farm he sees it all with a new eye. He still spends his days driving the manure wagon round a seven-acre field and driving harrows in a cloud of dust. But it is all different. He now knows what manure *is*. Before that he thought it was just manure. And he now understands why dust floats and he knows what he is doing when he pulverizes the soil, instead of merely thinking that he is "breaking it up good."

During this period of interregnum my father and mother lived at different places—Swanmore and Shoreham (in Sussex) and then Porchester. Their large family (which ultimately reached eleven in England and Canada) were born round in this way, only two in the same place of the six born in England. It was from Porchester that my father was sent out ahead of us by my grandfather to Kansas, a place of which my grandfather must have heard great things in the early seventies, though its first charm of the John Brown days was fading.

Porchester is the only place of my childhood days in England that I really remember. I lived there for two years (age four and a half to six and a half), and in a sense it still means the England that is England to me. At the opening of the present war, when the inspiring song "There'll Always Be an England" burst upon the world, I set forth this theme, as centred for me round Porchester in a magazine publication, which I reproduce here.

THE ENGLAND I REMEMBER
There'll Always Be an England

I imagine that somebody first said that away back in Anglo-Saxon times. The people who heard him say it most likely remarked, "Well, naturally!" and, "Poetic chap, eh?"

Yet when I first heard those words sung they brought back to me a sudden remembrance of the England of my childhood and a poignant affection for it, more than I knew I had. This, I am sure, happened to many people. . . .

ALWAYS BE AN ENGLAND

This, most certainly, is true of the immemorial village of Porchester in which I was brought up, for which the flight of time was meaningless. But my father's farm in South Africa, as I have said before, was eaten out by locusts, and so he and my mother came home, where I and other brothers were born.

Meantime my grandfather was consulting the map and picked on Kansas because at that time the railways only got that far. My father went first, and we were placed in Porchester so that we couldn't get to the Isle of Wight too often. We were ready to go to America when word came that my father's farm in Kansas had been eaten by grasshoppers (they are the same as locusts). This meant delay while my grandfather looked for something farther still. So we waited on in Porchester, and I had altogether six years of an English childhood that I had no right to have under the rules.

Porchester? Where is it? Right across the water from Portsmouth. What water? Ah, now, that I never knew—it's the water between Portsmouth and Porchester. You can tell it by the tall masts and yards of the men-of-war and of the *Victory* swinging there at anchor. . . . Up at the end of it was Paul's Grove, where St. Paul preached to the ancient—ah, there you have me—but to a congregation probably very like my uncle Charles's congregation in the little Porchester church. . . . The church stood—or it did in 1876, and things can hardly have changed in so short a time—inside the precincts of Porchester Castle. You've seen the castle, perhaps—a vast quadrangle of towers and battlements, and a great space inside. for cattle during sieges. The newer parts were built by the Normans but the original part by the Romans. The Normans built the church, but Good Queen Anne "restored" it, with a lot of others, and so, on the wall, there was a great painted lettering in gilt and faded colours: BY THE BOUNTY OF QUEEN ANNE. You could spell it out from your tall pew by the sunlight falling on the wall through the dancing leaves, while Uncle Charles preached, quietly so as not to wake the Normans, and the people gently dozed.

. . . ALWAYS, AN ENGLAND . . .

Why, of course, to the people of Porchester. Time left no trace there; all the centuries were yesterday, St. Paul, and the castle, and Queen Elizabeth's bedroom, and Uncle Charles and Queen Anne.

. . . WHEREVER THERE'S A BUSY STREET . . .

Busy? Well, I suppose you would call it busy, the village street with the little "common" breaking

24

it in the middle. There was only one of everything: one public house, one grocery, one rectory (Uncle Charles's), one windmill (Pyecroft's), one fly (Peacock's), and so on. There'd been no competition for years. The public house, the Crown and Anchor, stood where it should, where the streets came together at the "common," and looked as it should in *Father, Dear Father, Come Home with Me Now* . . . with red curtains in the windows.

. . . WHEREVER THERE ARE TURNING WHEELS . . .

Pyecroft's mill looked just right, standing down on the water a little way from the castle. The sails of Pyecroft's mill moved so slowly they seemed to soar and hover. Tennyson speaks of a "tall mill that whistled on the waste." He fell down there, eh, Pyecroft? Pyecroft looked the part admirably, all dust . . . and Peacock who had the fly matched it. All the people in Porchester looked like that; each fitted the part . . . Old General Hurdle coming down the street, a frail, old, soldierly figure, so upright that he quivered on his stick. Take old Grubb, who had been in the Navy in the Great War (what we called the Great War then); he sat catching periwinkles, or whatever they caught, where the castle moat drained into the sea. He looked it exactly, all tar. . . .

All the people, as I say, looked the part—the kind of things despaired of by the movies. I never knew whether Gilbert and Sullivan copied England or England copied Gilbert and Sullivan.

. . . *A MILLION MARCHING FEET* . . .

I am afraid that would be a large order for Porchester in 1876 . . . a million—well, perhaps it seemed so to us children when swarms of people used to come to the castle on holidays—I only half recall them, Whitmonday, something Wednesday, Coronation Day—with Aunt Sally's ginger beer and swings and drunken sailors.

. . . *RED, WHITE, AND BLUE* . . .

The blue, of course, was the sea. As for the "drunken sailors," why indeed shouldn't they be drunk? They were "ashore," weren't they? Those sailors were better drunk than sober . . . scattering pennies and full of fun. Now a soldier was different . . . a low sort of fellow, hanging around public houses and getting poor girls into trouble . . . Why isn't he off in Ashantee or someplace like that where soldiers belong?

. . . BRITONS, AWAKE . . .

Awake? Well, not too completely. I think of Uncle Charles preaching decorously, quietly, the congregation nodding. I wouldn't disturb that; it has been undisturbed too long. Uncle Charles— I have heard him say it—was singularly fortunate. In Porchester there was no outbreak of "religion." There was no chapel, no open-air preaching, no vulgar confession of sin. No people got sudden "salvation"; they got it gradually, through eighty years of drowsy Sundays. When I was six it all came to an end. My grandfather found a place called Upper Canada, clean out of reach of a railway. . . .

. . . WHAT DOES IT MEAN TO YOU? . . .

Then came the most vivid memory, saying goodbye to England as a child. . . . We went on board a great ship at Liverpool, a ship with the towering masts and rigging of the grand old days . . . went on board from a hole in the side, it seemed. It was all very wonderful to us, though lots of people, like my mother, cried, because going to America in 1876 meant good-bye.

But for us, the children, it was different; it was all wonderful . . . the crew and all the passengers joined to haul up the anchor . . . And they sang the song of the departing English, "Cheer, boys, cheer, no more of idle sorrow," that echoed down the decades. As the words died away on the ear— "Farewell, England, much as we have loved thee, courage, true hearts, will bear us on our way!"— the great ship was surging into the darkness under press of sail heading to what we call "America."

. . . SHOUT IT LOUD: THE EMPIRE TOO . . .

It was all fun for us . . . the wind, the waves, the magnificence of the "saloon" . . . And then the great sheets of ice until the ship stopped. On Sunday the clergyman prayed to have it taken away and it went.

Then came a morning when someone called

down the companionway, "Come and see America"
. . . And there it was, a tall, hard coast of trees and
rock, clear and bright in the sunshine, not a bit
soft, like England.

. . . IF ENGLAND MEANS AS MUCH
TO YOU . . .

It was the Gaspé coast, and we were entering the
St. Lawrence. I understand that one of the members who represents this section in a legislature pro-
poses to break away from England the three million
people of English race and birth, to say nothing of
the other three million British, who live in Canada.
It would be to blot out, for some, the memories of
childhood and, for all, the remembered talk of parents and old people . . . tear up the books that
hold the elegies in country churchyards, and hush
the sea songs of England on which Tom Bowling's
name floats to us down the wind.

Speaking of Porchester, I may say that after I
had gone down to Hambledon with E. V. Lucas
I was so fascinated with the role of the returned
native that I found time to make a hurried trip to

Porchester, to try it out again. When I got there I found my way from the station up (or down; you never know which they call it in England) the straggled street to the village common and to the Father-Dear-Father-Come-Home-with-Me-Now public house of which I spoke. I went into the Crown and Anchor and struck the proper attitude over a glass of beer at the bar. "Nearly fifty years ago," I said (feeling like the Silver King come home), "I used to live in this village. Perhaps you can tell me something about the people I remember."

The barmaid (she looked pretty ripe) threw her head indignantly in the air. "No indeed, I couldn't," she said. "The idear!"

I saw that I was in wrong. "Not you yourself," I said. "You weren't born and couldn't remember, but you may have heard of them from your—grandparents."

"Well," she said, mollified, "Grandfather's in behind now. You might come in and see him."

I went "in behind," and there was Grandfather looking just right, as everything does in Porchester, just exactly the part, seated in a chair, snow-white hair, a stick—age, say ninety.

"I thought perhaps," I said, "you could tell me something of the people I remember here fifty years ago."

"Eh?" he shouted.

So I saw I'd have to speed things up.

"Could you tell me anything about my uncle, the Reverend Charles Butler, who used to be the rector here fifty years ago?"

"The Reverend Charles Butler!" he shouted bitterly. "Indeed I could! There was the meanest man that ever came to this village. He'd-a stopped every poor man's beer, he would, if he'd had his way. Don't talk to me of the Reverend Charles Butler."

I decided not to.

So I went out and I managed to find the house where we lived when I was a child in Porchester. But what a poor, humble-looking place! I had no idea that it could have been as poor as that! A little "hall" just wide enough to squeeze through, a room on the left of it the size of a box—the "drawing room," I called it at once from memory—and another box behind it. I think my mother had the nerve to call it the "breakfast room." I felt hurt and humiliated coming out. I hadn't realized how used I had become to being well off, to living in comfort and having everything. As I came out I saw that there were some men there, evidently a builder and his "hands." They told me they were going to knock down the house. I told them to go right ahead.

After that I had no heart to go on and see the castle. It might have turned out to be just nothing as beside, say, the Royal York Hotel in Toronto or the Château Frontenac in Quebec.

It is better not to go back to the place you came from. Leave your memory as it is. No reality will ever equal it.

It was from my Hampshire childhood that I draw my interest in the American frigate *Chesapeake,* of which noble old ship I have a "chunk" on my library table.

Everyone recalls from his school history the immortal story of the great fight between the American frigate *Chesapeake* and the British frigate *Shannon* outside of Boston on June 1, 1813. It is not merely the victory of the *Shannon* that is remembered but the chivalrous nature of the conflict, the ships meeting after a courteous challenge from Captain Broke of the *Shannon* to Captain Lawrence of the *Chesapeake*. Broke generously offered to send any of his attendant vessels out of range of helping him. The ships were an even match—*Shannon*, 1,066 tons, broadside 544 pounds, crew 330; the *Chesapeake*, 1,135 tons, broadside 570, crew (about) 400.

The result of the battle was a complete victory for the *Shannon*, but with terrible loss on both sides. Lawrence was mortally wounded; Broke so desperately wounded as never to fully recover, though he lived to be an admiral and only died in 1841.

Now, I have always had a certain personal interest in the *Chesapeake*. I have, as I say, on my library table a "chunk" of very hard wood (teak or mahogany, I suppose), about eight inches by three inches by two and a half inches, that was originally a piece of the *Chesapeake*. I have had it for nearly seventy years, the kind of thing you never lose if you pay no attention to it, like the fidelity of an old friend.

When we were leaving England in 1876 to go to "America" we were taken over to the Isle of Wight to see my grandfather, who was naturally delighted —so much so that he gave me from the drawing-room table at Oak Hill this bit of wood and said, "That was a piece of the *Chesapeake*." Written on it in his writing, but now faded beyond recognition, were the words, *A Piece of the American Frigate "Chesapeake"—Captured 1813.*

I always wondered how my grandfather came to have a piece of the *Chesapeake*, and this gave me an interest in the fate of the vessel. But any printed account in the histories merely said that the *Chesapeake* was taken across the Atlantic to England— which is quite true—and was commissioned in the service of the Royal Navy—which is not so. But it has been only of late years, when I have been concerned with writing Canadian history, that I have been able to get full details of the fate of the old ship. I am indebted here very greatly to the library staff of the Boston Public Library.

The amazing thing is that the *Chesapeake* was taken over to England and is still there—all the best timbers of the vessel, built in solid as they came out of the ship, went into the making of a mill and are still throbbing and quivering all day as the mill, one hundred and twenty-three years old, still hums in an English village, grinding corn.

The mill is at Wickham, and if you don't know where Wickham is, I may say it's near Fareham—and Fareham?—well, close to Porchester—and Porchester?—well, that's where I lived in England. Anyway, all these places are in Hampshire, freely admitted to be (by all who live there) the noblest of the English counties.

So there's the mill, and nobody knows about it. The reason is that people who know all about the *Chesapeake* know nothing of Wickham and people who live in Wickham know nothing about the *Chesapeake,* though of course they all know about the old mill. If you said, "That mill was built out of the American ship *Chesapeake,* wasn't it?" they'd say, "Aye, like as not!"—meaning that that would be just the kind of thing to build a Hampshire mill out of.

Here is the story, though lack of space forbids full citation of authorities.

After the battle of the first of June the *Chesapeake* was sailed (or partly towed) to Halifax Harbour—a voyage of five days. She entered the harbour in the wake of the *Shannon* on June 6, presenting a terrible contrast of glory and tragedy, pride and honour—gay strings of bright flags of victory flying above battered ports and broken bulwarks, patched up as might be after the havoc of the broadsides.

Judge Haliburton, the famous writer still remembered for *Sam Slick*, went on board. "The *Chesapeake*," he wrote, "was like a charnel house . . . main deck filled with hammocks of the wounded, dead and dying . . . the deck had of necessity (heavy weather?) not been cleaned . . . steeped in gore as in a slaughterhouse." The body of Captain Lawrence, who had died on board, lay on the quarter-deck under the Stars and Stripes. He was buried, with many of his men, in Halifax.

The *Chesapeake*, refitted as might be, was sailed across to Portsmouth. There history loses her with the false lead that the Royal Navy recommissioned

the ship. This is not so, nor can I find any definite
authority to say that she ever sailed again. She was
bought as she stood for five hundred pounds by a
Mr. Holmes. He broke up the vessel, sold several
tons of copper from the sheeting with all fittings and
timber, and doubled his money. The main timbers were pitch pine, new and sound, and some of
them were sold for housebuilding in Portsmouth
but the best of them were bought by a Mr. John
Prior for two hundred pounds to build a mill. This
he duly erected (1820) in the hamlet of Wickham.
The main timbers of the deck, built into the structure intact, were (and are) thirty-two feet long and
eighteen inches square. The purloins were used,
just as they were, for joists.

With that the *Chesapeake* was forgotten, and
Wickham—it antedates the Norman Conquest—
fell asleep again.

Forty years later a descendant, or relation (I
cannot trace him), of Captain Broke of the *Shannon* got interested in gathering information. In a
memoir which he wrote he quotes a letter from
the Vicar of Fareham, date of 1864, with the information given above and the statement that the

timbers of the *Chesapeake* (in fact, the whole mill) seemed "good for centuries yet."

They talk in centuries in Hampshire.

Then comes another sleep.

Then a Hampshire *Gazetteer and Guide* of 1901 reports that the mill at Wickham made of the timbers of the *Chesapeake* is still intact and in active operation.

Then followed another sleep of the topic till in 1943 I woke it again by writing to the present Vicar of Fareham. I hadn't written sooner because, although I knew the *Chesapeake* was in a mill, I was looking for the mill to be on the Isle of Wight.

So I wrote to the Vicar of Fareham, who referred me to Mr. George Orwell of Fareham, who has done a lot of antiquarian work, especially in things concerning the Navy, and whose writings under the name of historian are well known to all people who love British antiquities (very fine people).

Mr. Orwell wrote me to say that the mill is still (April 4, 1943) quite as it was, timbers and all, going strong and likely to see a long while yet.

What ought to be done about it? These timbers of the deck of the *Chesapeake*—rebuilt into their earlier semblance—should have something of the sacred memory of the deck of the *Victory*. Why not buy them and give them to the United States? They should be a gift to the Naval Academy at Annapolis. Those who know that place will recall its trophies—the proudest part of the establishment. There swings still afloat the schooner *America* that won the cup in 1850 something, never recaptured; there is the old *Constitution* and the *Reina Mercedes,* and there in the great hall is Perry's flag with his *"Don't give up the ship,"* and much else.

The *Chesapeake* would build into a fine platform, the old deck reproduced, for Mr. Churchill to lecture from.

When I look back on this mid-Victorian England into which I was born and which first stamped itself on my mind, it gives me many things to think about. How deeply set it was in the mould in which England was cast and in which, to a great extent, it still remains. Side by side with all that is splendid in history and in character is that everlasting division that separates people from one another with the heavy ridges and barriers of class distinction. Here are people born to be poor, and how poor they were! I can remember that when we had done with our tea leaves old women (the place seemed full of them) would come and take them away to use over again. There were the poor and there were the half poor, and there were the respectable people and the genteel people, and the gentry and above them the great people, all the way to the queen. And they all knew their places.

There was an elementary school called a national school, where the children of the poor and of the respectable went at a fee of one penny a week. I can see now that it must have been one of the schools set up under the new Act, as it was then, of 1870, the first statute that ever gave England general primary education. England had got afraid that an illiterate population might mean danger to the nation. They had had the object lesson of the armies of the Civil War in America. The loud

laughter of the London *Times* and the haw! haw!
of the professional British officers had been ex-
changed for silent admiration and deep respect
when the same people realized what it means to
have an army of men every one of whom could
read and write, of skilled mechanics who could in-
terpret a printed diagram, and private soldiers with
the technical knowledge to repair a damaged loco-
motive and reset a dismantled telegraph line. It
had become plain enough that England had to do
what one of its statesmen of the moment called "ed-
ucate its masters," if only for the masters' sake.

That was seventy-five years ago. And strangely
enough the wheel has turned a full circle and a
similar discussion runs in the current journals of
1944. All through the present controversy over the
schools and how to make the public schools public
runs the note of anxiety, Are we really finding all
the brains of the nation? All, we need them all!
National brains are the first line of public safety
for everybody. There must be no gifted children
left too poor for their gifts to give service to the
nation. Scholarships, endowments, anything! We
must have them.

It is a wonderful change. Compare it with the sentiment of Gray's *Elegy*, in which the poet sorrows for the lack of opportunity that kept people down to the level of the poor and buried them in a country churchyard, but sorrows only for their own sakes.

Perhaps in this neglected spot is laid
  Some heart once pregnant with celestial fire;
Hands, that the rod of empire might have swayed,
  Or waked to ecstasy the living lyre.

With Gray the sentiment is as of a wishful luxurious pity and has nothing to do with any keen, anxious fear that the nation needs these men and must not bury them unknown. His very phrases show it: "waking the living lyre" is a thing that most of us could postpone for a while.

But, as I say, there was the national school functioning at a penny a week for the poor and the respectable. But for the genteel, no, not if they could reach a little higher, and of course not under any circumstances for the gentry. So two older brothers and I—aged nine and eight and six—went therefore to a dame's school, with which my academic education began in 1875, not to be completed till 1903 with a Chicago Ph.D. I recall but little of the dame school except the first lesson in geography, in which the dame held up a map and we children recited in chorus, "The top of the map is always the north, the bottom south, the right hand east, the left hand west!" I wanted to speak out and say, "But it's only that way because you're holding it that way," but I was afraid to. Cracks with a ruler were as easy to get in a dame's school as scratches down on the Rio Grande.

So, as I say, it was an England all of class and caste, with everybody doing his duty in the state of life into which it had pleased God to call him. But of this later.

LIFE ON THE
OLD FARM

I ENJOY the distinction, until very recently a sort of recognized title of nobility in Canada and the United States, of having been "raised on the old farm." Till recently, I say, this was the acknowledged path towards future greatness, the only way to begin. The biographies of virtually all our great men for three or four generations show them as coming from the farm. The location of the "old home farm" was anywhere from Nova Scotia to out beyond Iowa, but in its essence and idea it was always the same place. I once described it in a book of verse which I wrote as a farewell to economics, which was so clever that no one could read it and which I may therefore quote with novelty now.

The Homestead Farm, way back upon the Wabash,
Or on the Yockikenny,
Or somewhere up near Albany—the Charm
Was not confined to one, for there were many.

There when the earliest Streak of Sunrise ran,
The Farmer dragged the Horses from their Dream
With "Get up, Daisy" and "Gol darn yer, Fan,"
Had scarcely snapped the Tugs and Britching than
The furious Hayrack roared behind the team.
  All day the Hay
  Was drawn that way
  Hurled in the Mow
  Up high—and how!
Till when the ending Twilight came, the loaded
  Wain
With its last, greatest Load turned Home again.
  The Picture of it rises to his Eye
  Sitting beside his Father, near the Sky.

I admit that within the last generation or so, in softer times of multiplying luxury, men of eminence have been raised in a sickly sort of way in the cities themselves, have got their strength from high-school athletics, instead of at the woodpile and behind the harrows, and their mental culture by reading a hundred books once instead of one book a hundred times. But I am talking of an earlier day.

It was a condition, of course, that one must be raised on the old farm and then succeed in getting off it. Those who stayed on it turned into rustics, into "hicks" and "rubes," into those upstate characters which are the delight of the comic stage. You had your choice! Stay there and turn into a hick; get out and be a great man. But the strange thing is that they all come back. They leave the old farm as boys so gladly, so happy to get away from its dull routine, its meaningless sunrise and sunset, its empty fresh winds over its fields, the silence of the bush—to get away into the clatter and effort of life, into the crowd. Then, as the years go by, they come to realize that at a city desk and in a city apartment they never see the sunrise and the sunset, have forgotten what the sky looks like at night and where the Great Dipper is, and find nothing on the angry gusts of wind or the stifling heat of the city streets that corresponds to the wind over the empty fields . . . so they go back, or they think they do, back to the old farm. Only they rebuild it, but not with an ax but with an architect. They make it a great country mansion with flagstoned piazzas and festooned pergolas—and it isn't the old farm any more. You can't have it both ways.

But as I say, I had my qualifying share, six years of the old farm—after I came out as a child of six from England—in an isolation which in these days of radio and transport is unknown upon the globe.

As explained in the first chapter, I was brought out by my mother from England to Canada as the third of her six children in 1876 on the steamship *Sarmatian,* Liverpool to Montreal, to join my father who had gone ahead and taken up a farm. The *Sarmatian* was one, was practically the last one, of those grand old vessels of the Allan Line which combined steam with the towering masts, the cloud of canvas, the maze of ropes and rigging of a full-rigged three-masted ship. She was in her day a queen of the ocean, that last word which always runs on to another sentence. She had been built in 1871, had had the honour of serving the queen as a troopship for the Ashanti war and the further honour of carrying the queen's daughter to Canada as the wife of the Marquis of Lorne, the governor general. No wonder that in my recollection of her the *Sarmatian* seemed grand beyond belief and carried a wealth of memories of the voyage of which I have already spoken. For years I used to feel as if I would "give anything" to see the *Sarmatian* again. "Give anything" at that stage of my finance meant, say, anything up to five dollars— anyway, a whole lot. And then it happened years and years after, when I had gone to Montreal to teach at McGill (it was in 1902), that I saw in the papers that the *Sarmatian* was in port; in fact I found that she still came in regularly all season and would be back again before navigation closed. So I never saw her. I meant to but I never did. When I read a little later that the old ship had been broken up I felt that I would have "given anything" (ten dollars then) to have seen her.

In those days most people still came up, as we did in 1876, by river steamer from Montreal to Toronto. At Kingston we saw the place all decked with flags and were told that it was the "Twenty-fourth of May." We asked what that meant, because in those days they didn't keep "Queen's Birthday" as a holiday in England. They kept Coronation Day with a great ringing of bells, but whether there was any more holiday to it than bell ringing I don't remember. But, as we were presently to learn, the "Twenty-fourth" was at that time the great Upper Canada summer holiday of the year; Dominion Day was still too new to have got set. There wasn't any Labour Day or any Civic Holiday.

From Toronto we took a train north to Newmarket; a funny train, it seemed to us, all open and quite unlike the little English carriages, cut into compartments that set the fields spinning round when you looked out of the window. Newmarket in 1876 was a well-established country town—in fact, as they said, "quite a place." It still is. It was at that time the place from which people went by the country roads to the south side of Lake Simcoe, the township of Georgina, to which at that time there was no railway connection. From Newmarket my father and his hired man were to drive us the remaining thirty miles to reach the old farm. They had for it two wagons, a lumber wagon and a "light" wagon. A light wagon was lighter than a lumber wagon, but that's all you could say about it—it is like those histories which professors call "short" histories. They might have been longer. So away we went along the zigzag roads, sometimes along a good stretch that would allow the horses to break into a heavy attempt at a trot, at other times ploughing through sand, tugging uphill, or hauling over corduroy roads of logs through thick swamps where the willow and alder bushes almost met overhead and where there was "no room to pass." On the lift of the hills we could see about us a fine rolling country, all woods, broken with farms, and here and there in the distance on the north horizon great flecks of water that were Lake Simcoe. And so on, at a pace of four or five miles an hour, till as the day closed in we went over a tumbled bridge with a roaring milldam and beyond it a village, the village of Sutton—two mills, two churches, and quite a main street, with three taverns. My father told us that this was our own village, a gift very lightly received by us children after memories of Porchester and Liverpool and the *Sarmatian*. My

mother told me years afterwards that to her it was
a heartbreak. Beyond the village, my father told us,
we were on our home road—another dubious gift,
for it was as heavy as ever, with a great cedar
swamp a mile through in the centre, all corduroy
and willows and marsh and water; beyond that up
a great hill with more farmhouses, and so across
some fields, to a wind-swept hill space with a
jumble of frame buildings and log barns and out-
houses, and there we were at the old farm, on a
six-year unbroken sentence.

The country round our farm was new in the
sense that forty years before it was unbroken wild-
erness and old in the sense that farm settlers,
when they began to come, had come in quickly.
Surveyors had marked out roads. The part of the
bush that was easy to clear was cleared off in one
generation, log houses built, and one or two frame
ones, so that in the sense the country in its outline
was just as it is now: only at that time it was more
bush than farms, now more farms than the
shrunken remnant of bush. And of course in 1876
a lot of old primeval trees, towering hemlocks and

birch, were still standing. The last of the great bush fires that burned them out was in the summer when we came, the bush all burning, the big trees falling in masses of spark and flame, the sky all bright, and the people gathered from all round to beat out the shower of sparks that fell in the stubble fields . . .

This country around Lake Simcoe (we were four miles to the south of it and out of the sight of it), beautiful and fertile as it is, had never been settled in the old colonial days. The French set up missions there among the Hurons (northwest of the lake), but they were wiped out in the great Iroquois massacre of 1649 in the martyrdom of the Fathers Lalemant and Brébeuf. The tourist of to-day sees from his flying car the road signs of "Martyr's Shrine" intermingled with the "Hot Dogs" and "Joe's Garage." After the massacre the French never came back. The Iroquois danger kept the country empty, as it did all western Ontario. Nor did the United Empire Loyalists come here. They settled along the St. Lawrence and the Bay of Quinte and Niagara and Lake Erie, but the Lake

Simcoe country remained till that century closed as empty as it is beautiful.

Settlement came after the "Great War" ended with Waterloo and world peace, and a flock of British emigrants went out to the newer countries. Among them were many disbanded soldiers and sailors and officers with generous grants of land. These were what were called in England "good" people, meaning people of the "better" class but not good enough to stay at home, which takes money. With them came adherents and servants and immigrants at large, but all good people in the decent sense of the word, as were all the people round our old farm no matter how poor they were. The entry of these people to the Lake Simcoe country was made possible by Governor Simcoe's opening of Yonge Street, north from Toronto to the Holland River. It was at first just a horse track through the bush, presently a rough roadway connecting Toronto (York) with the Holland River, and then, by cutting the corner of Lake Simcoe with the Georgian Bay and thus westward to the Upper Lakes, a line of communication safe from American invasion. It was part of Governor Simcoe's preoccupation over the defense of Upper Canada, which bore such good fruit in its unforeseen results of new settlement.

So the settlers, once over the waters of Lake Simcoe, found their way along its shore, picked out the likely places, the fine high ground, the points overlooking the lake. Here within a generation arose comfortable lake-shore homes, built by people with a certain amount of money, aided by people with no money but glad to work for wages for a time, till they could do better. From the first the settlement was cast in an aristocratic mould such as had been Governor Simcoe's dream for all his infant colony. Simcoe was long since gone by this time. He left Canada in 1796 and died in England in 1806. But the mark that he set on Upper Canada wore faint only with time and is not yet obliterated. Simcoe planned a constitution and a colony to be an "image and transcript" of England itself. An established church and an aristocracy must be the basis of it. To Simcoe a democrat was a dangerous Jacobin and a dissenter a snivelling hypocrite. He despised people who would sit down to eat with their own servants, as even "good" people began to do in Upper Canada; "Fellows of one table," he called them, and he wanted nothing to do with them in his government. Others shared his views, and hence that queer touch of make-believe, or real aristocracy, that was then characteristic of Simcoe's York (Toronto) and that helped to foster the Canadian rebellion of 1837.

So after the first "aristocracy" houses were built on the lake shore of Georgina Township settlers began to move up to the higher ground behind it, better land and cheaper. For the lake, for being on the water, most of them cared nothing. They wanted to get away from it. The lake shore was cold. It is strange to think that now you can buy all of that farmland you want at about thirty or forty dollars an acre, but an acre down at the lake shore is worth, say, a couple of thousand, and you can't get it anyway.

Our own farm with its buildings was, I will say, the damnedest place I ever saw. The site was all right, for the slow slope of the hillside west and south gave a view over miles of country and a view of the sunset only appreciated when lost. But the house! Someone had built a cedar log house and then covered it round with clapboard, and then someone else had added three rooms stuck along the front with more clapboard, effectually keeping all the sunlight out. Even towards the sunset there were no windows, only the half glass top of a side door. A cookhouse and a woodshed were stuck on behind. Across a grass yard were the stable, cedar logs plastered up, and the barns, cedar logs loose and open, and a cart shed and a henhouse, and pigsties and all that goes with a farm. To me as a child the farm part seemed just one big stink. It does still: the phew! of the stable—not so bad as the rest; the unspeakable cowshed, sunk in the dark below a barn, beyond all question of light or ventilation, like a mediæval oubliette; the henhouse, never cleaned and looking like a guano-deposit island off the coast of Chile, in which the hens lived if they could and froze dead if they couldn't; the pigsties, on the simple Upper Canada fashion of a log pen and a shelter behind, about three feet high. Guano had nothing on them.

We presently completed our farmhouse to match

the growing family by adding a new section on the far side of it, built of frame lumber only, with lath and plaster and no logs, thin as cardboard and cold as a refrigerator. Everything froze when the thermometer did. We took for granted that the water would freeze in the pitchers every night and the windowpanes cover up with frost, not that the old farm was not heated. It had had originally a big stone fireplace in the original log house, but as with all the fireplaces built of stone out of the fields without firebrick, as the mortar began to dry out the fireplace would set the house on fire. That meant getting up on the roof (it wasn't far) with buckets of water and putting it out. My father and the hired man got so tired putting out the house on fire that we stopped using the fireplace and had only stoves, box stoves that burned hemlock, red hot in ten minutes with the dampers open. You could be as warm as you liked, according to distance, but the place was never the same two hours running. There were, I think, nine stoves in all; cutting wood was endless. I quote again from my forgotten book.

Winter stopped not the Work; it never could.
Behold the Furious Farmer splitting Wood.
The groaning Hemlock creaks at every Blow
"Hit her again, Dad, she's just got to go."
                    And up he picks
                    The Hemlock sticks
                    Out of the snow.

For light we had three or four coal-oil lamps, but being just from England, where they were unknown, we were afraid of them. We used candles made on the farm from tallow poured into a mould, guttering damn things, to be snuffed all the time and apt to droop over in the middle. It is hardly credible to me now, but I know it is a fact that when my brother and I sat round a table doing our lessons or drawing and painting pictures, all the light we had was one tallow candle in the middle of the table. It should have ruined our eyesight, but it didn't. I don't think any of us under fifty wore spectacles; just as the ill-cooked food of the farm, the heavy doughy bread, the awful pork and pickles should have ruined our digestions but couldn't. Boys on the farm who go after the cattle at six in the morning are in the class of the iron dogs beside a city step.

My father's farm—one hundred acres, the standard pattern—was based on what is called mixed farming—that is, wheat and other grains, hay, pasture, cattle, a few sheep and pigs and hens, roots for winter, garden for summer and wood to cut in the bush. The only thing to sell was wheat, the false hope of the Ontario farmer of the seventies, always lower in the yield than what one calculated (if you calculated low it went lower) and always (except once in a happy year) lower than what it had to be to make it pay. The other odd grains we had to sell brought nothing much, nor the cattle, poor lean things of the prebreeding days that survived their awful cowshed. My father knew nothing about farming, and the hired man, "Old Tommy," a Yorkshireman who had tried a bush farm of his own and failed, still less. My father alternated furious industry with idleness and drinking, and in spite of my mother having a small income of her own from England, the farm drifted onto the rocks and the family into debt. Presently there was a mortgage, the interest on which being like a chain around my father's neck, and later on mine. Indeed, these years of the late 1870s were the hard times of Ontario farming, with mortgages falling due like snowflakes.

Farming in Ontario, in any case, was then and still is an alternating series of mortgages and prosperity following on like the waves of the sea. Anyone of my experience could drive you through the present farm country and show you (except that it would bore you to sleep) the mark of the successive waves like geological strata. Here on our right is the remains of what was the original log house of a settler: you can tell it from the remains of a barn, because if you look close you can see that it had a top story, or part of one, like the loft where Abraham Lincoln slept. You will see, too, a section of its outline that was once a window. Elsewhere, perhaps on the same farm, but still standing, is an old frame house that was built by mortgaging the log house. This one may perhaps be boarded up and out of use because it was discarded when wheat went to two dollars and fifty cents a bushel in the Crimean War and the farmer, suddenly enriched, was able to add another mortgage and built a brick house—those real brick houses that give the motorist the impression that all farmers are rich. So they were—during the Crimean War. Later on, and reflecting the boom years of the closing nineties and the opening century, are the tall hip-roofed barns with stone and cement basements below for cattle and silos at the side, which give the impression that all farmers are scientists—only they aren't; it's just more mortgages.

Such has been the background of Ontario farming for one hundred years.

Our routine on the farm, as children, was to stay on it. We were too little to wander, and even the nearest neighbours were half a mile away. So we went nowhere except now and then, as a treat, into Sutton village, and on Sunday to the church on the lake shore. Practically, except for school, we stayed at home all the time—years and years.

There was, a mile away, a school (School Section No. 3, Township of Georgina) of the familiar type of the "little red schoolhouse" that has helped to make America. It was a plain frame building, decently lighted, with a yard and a pump and a woodpile, in fact all the accessories that went with the academic life of School Section No. 3. The boys and girls who went there were the children of decent people (there were no others in the township), poor, but not exactly aware of it. In summer the boys went barefoot. We didn't—a question of caste and thistles. You have to begin it at three years old to get the feel for it.

There were two teachers, a man teacher and a lady teacher, and it was all plain and decent and respectable, and the education first class, away ahead of the dame-school stuff in England. All of the education was right to the point—reading, spelling, writing, arithmetic, geography—with no fancy, silly subjects such as disfigure our present education even at its beginning and run riot in the college at the top. Things about the school that were unsanitary were things then so customary that even we children from England found nothing wrong. We spit on our slates to clean them with the side of our hand. We all drank out of the same tin mug in the schoolyard. The boys and girls were together in classes, never outside.

The only weak spot in the system of the little red schoolhouse was that the teachers were not permanent, not men engaged in teaching making it their lifework, like the Scottish "dominie" who set his mark upon Scotland. You can never have a proper system of national education without teachers who make teaching their lifework, take a pride in it as a chosen profession, and are so circumstanced as to be as good as anybody—I mean as anything around. In the lack of this lies the great fault in our Canadian secondary education, all the way up to college.

So it was with the country schools of 1876. The teachers were young men who came and went, themselves engaged in the long stern struggle of putting themselves through college, for which their teaching was only a steppingstone. An arduous struggle it was. A schoolteacher (they were practically all men; the girl teachers were just appendages to the picture) got a salary of three hundred dollars to four hundred dollars a year. Call it four hundred dollars. During his ten months a year of teaching he paid ten dollars a month for his board and washing. I don't suppose that his clothes cost him more than fifty dollars a year, and all his other extras of every kind certainly not more than another fifty. For in those days, after necessaries were paid for, there was nothing to spend money on. The teacher never drank. Not that he didn't want to, but every drink cost money, five cents, and he hadn't got it. If a teacher did begin to drink and did start to loaf around the taverns, it undermined the sternness of his life's purpose as a slow leak undermines a dam. It became easier to drink than to save money; he felt rich instead of poor, and presently, as the years went by, he drank himself out of this purpose altogether, quit school-teaching, went north—to the lumber shanties or worked in a sawmill—living life downhill, marked out still, by the wreck of his education, as a man who had once been a teacher and still quoted poetry when he was tight.

But most, practically all, stuck right at it, saving, say, two hundred dollars a year towards college. And this is what college cost, college being the University of Toronto. The fees were forty dollars a year (say sixty dollars in medicine), and board and lodging in the mean drab houses of the side streets where the poorer students lived cost three dollars a week, and washing, I think, twenty-five cents a week. They washed anything then for five cents, even a full-dress shirt, and anyway the student hadn't got a full-dress shirt. College books in those days cost about ten dollars a year. There were no college activities that cost money, nothing to join that wanted five dollars for joining it, no cafeterias to spend money in, since a student ate three times a day at his boardinghouse and that was the end of it. There was no money to be spent on college girls, because at that time there were no college girls to spend money on. Homer says that the beauty of Helen of Troy launched a thousand ships (meaning made that much trouble). The attraction of the college girl was to launch about a thousand dollars —added to college expenses.

But all that was far, far away in 1876, and a student's college budget for the eight months of the session, including his clothes and his travel expenses and such extras as even the humblest and sternest must incur, would work out at about three hundred dollars for each college year. That meant that what he could save in a year and a half of teaching would give him one year at college. Added to this was the fact that in the vacation—the two months of a teacher's vacation or the four months for a college vacation—he could work on a farm for his board and twenty dollars a month and save almost the whole of the twenty dollars. I have known at least one teacher, later on a leader of the medical profession of Alberta, who put in seven years of this life of teaching to get his college course. But in most cases there would be some extra source of supply: an uncle who owned a sawmill and could lend two or three hundred dollars, or an uncle over in the States, or an older brother who came down from the "shanties" in the spring with more money than he knew what to do with. For what could he do with it, except drink or go to college?

So in the end adversity was conquered, and the teachers passed through college and into law or medicine, with perhaps politics and public life, and added one more name to the roll of honour of men who "began as teachers." Some failed on the last

lap, graduated, and then got married, tired of waiting for life to begin, and thus sank back again on
teaching—as a high-school teacher, a better lot but
still not good enough.

But the system was, and is, all wrong. Our
teacher, with his thirty dollars a month, didn't get
as much as our Old Tommy, the hired man, for he
and his wife had twenty dollars a month and a cottage with it and a garden, milk and eggs and vegetables and meat to the extent of his end (I forget
which) of any pig that was killed. A teacher situated like that could be a married man, as snug and
respected as a Scottish dominie with his cottage
and his kailyard, his trout rod and his half dozen
Latin books bound in vellum—"as good as anybody," which is one of the things that a man has
got to be in life if he is to live at all. The teachers
weren't. I never was, and never felt I was, in the
ten years I was a teacher. That is why later on I
spent so many words in decrying schoolteaching as
a profession, not seeing that schoolteaching is all
right for those who are all right for it. The thing
wrong is the setting we fail to give it.

Such was our school at School Section No. 3, Township of Georgina, County of York. It had also its amenities as well as its work. Now and again there were school "entertainments." I can't remember if the people paid to come. I rather think not, because in that case they wouldn't come. For an entertainment the school was lit with extra lamps. The teacher was chairman. The trustees made speeches or shook their heads and didn't. The trustees were among the old people who had come out from the "old country" with some part of another environment, something of an older world, still clinging to them. Some, especially Scotsmen like old Archie Riddell, would rise to the occasion and make a speech with quite a ring and a thrill to it, all about Marmion and Bruce and footprints on the sands of time. Then the teachers would say that we'd hear from Mr. Brown, and Mr. Brown, sitting in a sunken lump in a half-light, would be seen to shake his head, to assure us that we wouldn't. After which came violin music by local fiddlers, announced grandiloquently by the chairman as "Messrs. Park and Ego," although we knew that really they were just Henry Park and

Angus Ego. Perhaps also some lawyer or such person from the village four miles away would drive up for the entertainment and give a reading or a recitation. It was under those circumstances that I first heard W. S. Gilbert's *Yarn of the "Nancy Bell."* It seemed to me wonderful beyond words, and the Sutton lawyer, a man out of wonderland.

But going to the country school just didn't work out. It was too far for us, and in rough weather and storm impossible, and it was out of the question for a younger section of the family (the ones in between the baby and ex-baby and the "big boys"). Moreover, my mother was haunted with the idea that if we kept on at the school we might sideslip and cease to be gentlemen. Already we were losing our Hampshire accent, as heard in *Twinkle, Twinkle, Little Star*—not "stah," and not "star," but something in between. I can still catch it if I am dead tired or delirious. We were beginning also to say "them there" and "these here," and "who all" and "most always," in short, phrases that no one can use and grow up a gentleman.

So my mother decided that she would teach us herself and with characteristic courage set herself at it, in the midst of all her other work with the baby and the little children and the kitchen and the servants and the house. Servants, of course, we always had: at least one maid—I beg pardon, I'm losing my language—I mean one "hired girl" and a "little girl" and generally an "old woman." Top wages were eight dollars a month; a little girl got five dollars. There was a certain queer gentility to it all. The hired men never sat down to eat with us, nor did the hired girl. Her status, in fact, as I see it in retrospect, was as low and humble as even an English earl could wish it. She just didn't count.

My mother had had in England a fine education of the Victorian finishing-school type and added to it a love and appreciation of literature that never left her all her life, not even at ninety years of age. So she got out a set of her old English schoolbooks that had come with us in a box from England—

Colenso's *Arithmetic,* and Slater's *Chronology,* and Peter Parley's *Greece and Rome,* and Oldendorf's *New Method of French*—and gathered us around her each morning for school, opened with prayers, and needing them. But it was no good; we wouldn't pay attention, we knew it was only Mother. The books didn't work either—most of them were those English manuals of history and such, specially designed for ladies' schools and for ladies who had to teach their own children out in the "colonies." They were designed to get a maximum of effect for a minimum of effort, and hence they consisted mostly of questions and answers, the questions being what lawyers call leading questions, ones that suggest their own answers. Thus they reduced Roman history to something like this:

Q. Did not Julius Caesar invade Britain?

A. He did.

Q. Was it not in the year 55 B.C.?

A. It was.

Q. Was he not later on assassinated in Rome?

A. He was.

Q. Did not his friend Brutus take a part in assassinating him?

A. He did.

In this way one could take a birdlike flight over ancient history. I think we hit up about two hundred years every morning, and for ancient Egypt over one thousand years. I had such a phenomenal memory that it was all right for me, as I remembered the question and answer both. But my elder brothers Dick and Jim were of heavier academic clay, and so they just—as the politicians say—took it as read.

The *Arithmetic* of Bishop Colenso of Natal was heavier going. After multiplication and division it ran slap-bang into the Rule of Three, and Mother herself had never understood what the Rule of Three was, and if you went on beyond it all you found was Practice and Aliquot Parts. I know now that all this is rule-of-thumb arithmetic, meant for people who can't reason it out, and brought straight down from the Middle Ages to Colenso. The glory of the unitary method, whereby if one man needs ten cigarettes a day then two men need twenty, and so on for as many men and as many cigarettes and as long a time as you like—this had not dawned on the British mind. I think it was presently imported from America.

So my mother's unhappy lessons broke down, and we were just about to be sent back to the red schoolhouse when by good luck we managed to secure a family tutor, from whom we received, for the next three or four years, teaching better than I have ever had since and better than any I ever gave in ten years as a schoolteacher. Our tutor was a young man off a near-by farm, stranded halfway through college by not having taught long enough and compelled to go back to teaching. So my grandfather from England put up the money (for fear, of course, that we might come back home on him), and there we were with a tutor and a schoolroom, inkwells, scribblers, slates—in fact, a whole academic outfit. Our tutor was known as "Harry Park" to his farm associates, but to us, at once and always, as "Mr. Park," and he ranked with Aristotle in dignity and width of learning. Never have I known anyone who better dignified his office, made more of it, so that our little schoolroom was as formal as Plato in his Academy could have wished it. Mr. Park rechristened my brother Jim as "James," to give him class, and Dick reappeared as "Arthur." The hours were as regular as the clock itself, in fact more so, since Mr. Park's watch soon took precedence over the kitchen clock, as the "classes" (made up of us four boys and my little sister, just qualified) were as neatly divided as in a normal school. I had to be Class I, but my brothers didn't care, as they freely admitted that I was the "cleverest"—they looked on it as no great asset. For certain purposes, poetry and history, we were all together.

For us "Mr. Park" knew everything, and I rather think that he thought this himself. Ask him anything and we got the answer. "Mr. Park, what were the Egyptians like?" He knew it and he told it, in measured formal language.

Under "Mr. Park's" teaching my brothers at least learned all that could be put into them, and I personally went forward like an arrow. At eleven years of age I could spell practically anything, knew all there was to know of simple grammar (syntax, parsing, analysis), beyond which there is nothing worth while anyway, knew Collier's *British His-*

tory and *History of English Literature,* all the geography of all the countries including Canada (the provinces of Canada which had not been in Mother's book), and in arithmetic had grasped the unitary system and all that goes with it and learned how to juggle with vulgar fractions even when piled up like a Chinese pagoda, and with decimals let them repeat as they would.

After Mr. Park came to us as tutor and the little red schoolhouse of School Section No. 3, Township of Georgina, was cut out, our isolation was all the more complete. We practically stayed on the farm. But of course a part of the old farm, to children of eight to twelve years old, newly out from England, was a land of adventure; all the main part of it, as it sloped away to the south and west, was clear fields of the seven-acre pattern with snake fences all round it, piles of stones that had been cleared off the fields lying in the fence corners, raspberry bushes choking up the corners, but here and there an old elm tree springing up in an angle of the fence as a survival of the cleared forests. Elm trees have the peculiarity that they can do well alone, as no storm can break them, whereas hemlocks isolated by themselves are doomed. Hence the odd elm trees scattered all through this part of central Ontario, as if some-one had set them on purpose to serve as shade trees or landscape decoration. Heaven knows no one did. For the earlier settlers' trees, to a great extent, were the enemy. The Upper Canada forest was slaughtered by the lumber companies without regard for the future, which in any case they could neither foresee nor control. In the early days the export of lumber was only in the form of square timber—great sticks of wood from twelve to eight-een inches each way, not cut up into the boards and deals and staves of the later lumber trade. Hence the trees were squared as they fell in the falling forest, and about one third of the main tree and all its branches burned up as litter to get rid of it. That was the early settlers' idea of the bush: get rid of it where he could, and where it lay too low, too sunken, too marshy, to clear it. Then cut out the big trees and haul them out, leave the rest of the bushes there, and let farm clearings and roads get round it as best they could. As to plant-ing any new trees to conserve the old ones, the farmers would have thought it a madman's dream. The only trees planted were the straight, fast-growing Lombardy poplars, still seen in their old age, set out in single or in little rows in front of the early Ontario houses. These owe their origin to the legend or the fact that they act as lightning conductors, a part of Benjamin Franklin's legacy to North America, along with the box stove and much else.

I am saying then that our old farm at its north end fell slap away down a steep hillside at the foot of which began the bush that spread off sideways in both directions as far as one could see, and directly in front it rose again in a slope that blotted out all view of Lake Simcoe four miles away. Along the fringes of it were still some of the giant hemlocks that had escaped the full fury of the last bush fire, dead, charred, and still standing, but falling one by one. The bush, as one tried to penetrate it, grew denser and denser, mostly underbrush with tangled roots and second growth sprung up after the fires. It was so dense that for us it was impenetrable, and we ventured our way farther and farther in, carrying hatchets and alert for wildcats, which I am practically certain were not there, and for bears, which had left years and years ago.

We had hardly any social life, as we were prevented, partly by "class" and mainly by distance, from going over to the other farms after dark. To one farm where lived a family of English children of something the same mixed antecedents as ourselves we sometimes went over for tea, and at times all the way to the village or to the lake-shore houses. But such treks meant staying overnight.

So mostly we stayed at home, and in the evenings we did our lessons, if we had lessons to do, and my mother read to us Walter Scott and carried us away to so deep an impression of the tournaments and battlefields of the Crusade and of the warring forests of Norman-Saxon England that any later "moving picture" of such things is but a mere blur of the surface. We cannot have it both ways. Intensity of mental impression and frequency of mental impression cannot go together. Robinson Crusoe's discovery of Friday's footprints on the sand—read aloud thus by candlelight to wondering children—has a dramatic "horror" to it (horror means making one's hair stand up) that no modern cinema or stage can emulate. Similarly I recall the reading aloud of *Tom Sawyer,* then of course, still a new book, and the dramatic intensity of the disclosure that Indian Joe is sealed up in the great cave.

Our news from the outside world came solely in the form of the *Illustrated London News* sent out by my grandmother from England. In it we saw the pictures of the Zulu War and the (second) Afghan War and of Majuba Hill. With it we kept alive the British tradition that all Victorian children were brought up in, never doubting that of course the Zulus were wrong and the Afghans mistaken and the Boers entirely at fault. This especially, as Mother had lived in South Africa and said so.

On one point, however, of British Victorian orthodox faith I sideslipped at eight years old and have never entirely got back, and that too the greatest point in all British history. I refer to the question of George Washington and George the

Third and whether the Americans had the right to set up a republic. It so happened that there came to our farm for a winter visit an English cousin of my father's who had become (I do not know how, for it must have been a rare thing in the seventies) a female doctor in Boston. She used to tell me, while Jim and Dick were mucking out the chores in the barnyard, which was their high privilege, about the United States and the Revolution, and when she saw how interested I was she sent to Boston and got a copy of Colonel Thomas Wentworth Higginson's *Young Folks' (or People's) History of the United States*. There it was, pictures and all—General Gage and the Boston Boys (very neat boys and a very neat general), Washington crossing the Delaware (hard going), Washington taking command at Cambridge. "Cousin Sophy" used to read it out loud to us—a needed rest for Walter Scott—and we were all fascinated with it, Jim and Dick with the pictures and the soldiers, but I chiefly from the new sense of the burning injustice of tyranny, a thing I had never got from history before.

Forthwith the theory of a republic, and the

theory of equality, and the condemnation of hereditary rights seemed obvious and self-evident truths, as clear to me as they were to Thomas Jefferson. I stopped short at the queen partly, I suppose, because one touched there on heaven and hell and the church service and on ground which I didn't propose to tread. But for me, from then on, a hereditary lord didn't have a leg to stand on. In the sixty years (nearly seventy) since elapsed I have often tried to stand up hereditary peers again (I mean as members of a legislature), but they won't really stay up for me. I have studied it all, and lectured on it all, and written about it all. I know all about the British idea that if a thing had existed for a long time, and if most people like it and if it seems to work well and if it brings no sharp edge of cruelty and barbarity such as the world has learned again, then it is silly to break away from established institution on the ground of a purely theoretical fault. But I can't get by with the arguments. I broke with the House of Lords, with its hereditary peers and its bishops voting because they are bishops in 1879—or whenever it was—and the breech has never been really healed. People from

India have told me that no matter how scientific an education you may smear over an Indian doctor or scientist, put him in any emergency or danger and back he comes to his first beliefs: away goes medicine in favour of incantation and charms, and science abandons its instruments and its metric measurement and harks back a thousand years to astrology and mysticism.

I'm like that with my underlying Jeffersonian republicanism: back I slip to such crazy ideas as that all men are equal, and that hereditary rights (still saving out the British monarch) are hereditary wrongs.

Occasional treats broke the routine of our isolation on the farm, such as going into Sutton village for the "Twenty-fourth" (of May), the great annual holiday, or to see cricket matches between Sutton and other places, such as Newmarket, within cricket reach. For up to that time cricket still remained the game of the Upper Canada countryside, the game living on strong as against the competition of Yankee baseball and dying hard. At present cricket has shrunken in on Toronto and a few larger cities and school centres. But in the seventies and eighties it was everywhere. The wonder is, though, that it could survive at all—it makes such heavy demands—a decent "pitch" of prepared ground, without which the game is worthless, an outfield not too rough, and even for decent practice a certain minimum of players; while cricket "at the nets" is poor stuff without a good pitch and good bowling, especially if you haven't any nets. Nor can you have a real "match" at cricket without a real side of eleven or something close to it. Baseball, on the other hand, is quick and easy and universal. It can be played in a cow pasture or behind the barnyard or in the village street; two people can "knock out flies" and three can play at "rolling over the bat," and if you can't get nine for a game, a pitcher, catcher, and baseball will do—what's more, the game can be played out in an afternoon, an hour, or a minute. The wonder is that the British settlers in Upper Canada kept doggedly on with their British cricket as against the facile Yankee baseball and the indigenous lacrosse. I am quite sure that in the township of Georgina no one had ever seen the latter game in 1880.

Rarest and most striking of all treats was to be taken on a trip to Toronto on the new railway, which reached Lake Simcoe from the south by a branch line of the Toronto and Lake Nipissing Railway extended from Stouffville to Sutton and Jackson's Point Wharf (on the lake). It was part of that variegated network of little railways—of varied gauges and plans, all crooked as country roads, all afraid of a hill, and all trying to keep close to a steamer dock, each under different ownerships—which represents the shortsighted railway building of Ontario. Shortsighted? And yet I suppose it was hard to see ahead at all, in a community that stumbled and fell with every new onslaught of bad times and fought stubbornly against its forests and its torrents—half strangled in its own opportunity.

The completion of the railway and the arrival of the first train was a great event, much ringing of bells and blowing of whistles; then the train itself arrived by the sash factory and the gristmill.

It made a great difference, too, with commodities, such as coal and oranges, seen in Sutton for the first time. But, as with most town and village advances of that date, it just went so far and then stopped. Sutton fell asleep again and woke only to the sound of the motor horn and the advent of the tourist, in another world years later.

But for us children a trip on the train to Toronto, a treat that was accorded to each of us about twice in the next three years, was a trip into wonderland —England had grown dim. Toronto, even the Toronto I describe in the next chapter, was marvellous beyond all description.

But the most real of our standing treats and holidays came to us on contact with Lake Simcoe. This grew out of our going to church every Sunday in summer to the Lake Shore Church four miles away. To our farm equipment there had been added a "phaeton" for Mother to drive and the kind of horse that is driven in a phaeton, which is born quiet, never grows old, and lives on into eternity. The ease and comfort of a phaeton can be appreciated by riding once in a buckboard (just once is all you need), a vehicle that means a set of slats on axles, with a seat on the slats. Its motion is similar to that of the new "seasickness medicine." A phaeton with steel springs, low entrance, and two seats can carry a capacity load and attain a speed, on the level, of six miles an hour. Even at that we walked in turns.

The parish church of Georgina stood on the high bank dotted with cedar trees overlooking Lake Simcoe, and oh! what a paradise the view presented. I have often and often and often written of Lake Simcoe, I know, with a few odd miles left out here and there, its every stick and stone, its island and points, and I claim that there is in all the world no more beautiful body of water. Writing it up years ago in a Canadian *Geographical Journal*, I said:

"The islands of the Aegean Sea have been regarded for centuries as a scene of great beauty; I know, from having seen them, that the Mediterranean coast of France and the valleys of the Pyrenees are a charm to the enchanted country; and I believe that for those who like that kind of thing there is wild grandeur in the Highlands of Scotland, and a majestic solitude where the midnight sun flashes upon the ice peaks of Alaska. But to my thinking none of those will stand comparison with the smiling beauty of the waters, shores, and bays of Lake Simcoe and its sister lake, Couchiching. Here the blue of the deeper water rivals that of the Aegean; the sunlight flashes back in lighter colour from the sand bar on the shoals; the passing clouds of summer throw moving shadows as over a ripening field, and the mimic gales that play over the surface send curling caps of foam as white as ever broke under the bow of the Aegean galley.

"The Aegean is old. Its islands carry the crumbling temples of Homer's times. But everywhere its vegetation has been cut and trimmed and gardened by the hand of man. Simcoe is far older. Its forest outline is still what Champlain saw, even then unchanged for uncounted centuries. Look down through the clear water at the sunken trees that lie in the bay southeast of Sibbald's Point. They sank, as others sank before them, a hundred years ago; no hand of man has ever moved or touched them. The unquarried ledges of Georgina Island stood as they stand now when the Greeks hewed stone from the Pentelicus to build the Parthenon."

The whole point of our going to church on the lake shore on summer mornings was that we were allowed, by a special dispensation from the awful Sunday rules we were brought up on, to go in for a swim and to stick around beside the lake for an hour or so. The spot was one of great beauty. The earliest settlers had built a wooden church among the cedar trees, and in the very years of which I speak it was being replaced by the Lake Shore Church of cut stone that is one of the notable landmarks of the scenery of the district. It was built by the members of the Sibbald family, one of the chief families of the district, whose sons had gone abroad for service in the British Army and Navy and in India and, returning (in our day) as old men enriched in fortune and experience, built the stone church still standing as a memorial to their mother. A Latin motto (which outclassed me at nine years old) cut in a memorial stone on the face of the tower commemorates the fact. The church was built during two of our summers of churchgoing and swimming. The masons were not there on Sundays, but we could follow its progress every Sunday, in the stones new drilled for blasting, in the fresh-cut completed stones, and then in the rising layers of the walls, the upsweep of the tall roof (one Sunday to the next), the glass, the slates, and then—all of a sudden, as it were— we were singing in it.

Better still was it when my mother, a year or two later, 1880, was able to take a "summer cottage" near the church for a holiday of a month or so. "Summer cottage" is a courtesy title. It was an old log building built as a "parsonage," which in time proved unfit for habitation even by the meekest parson. But for a summer habitation it did well enough, and with it the glory of the lake and of the return to the water, which we lost since Porchester. We were like Viking children back to the sea! So will you find any British children, used to sight and sound of the sea, shut from the water a brief space in some inland or prairie town but exulting to get back to their agelong heritage. So were we with Lake Simcoe: making rafts of logs and boards before we had a boat, blown out to sea on our rafts and rescued, and thus learning what an offshore wind means—a thing that even today few Lake Ontario summer visitors understand. After rafts a flat-bottomed boat, liberally plugged up with hot pitch, then an attempt at making a sail and discovering that a flat-bottomed boat is no good—and so on, repeating the life of man on the ocean as the human race repeats in the individual its every stage of evolution.

In my case Lake Simcoe was a more interesting field of navigation then than now, more real. It is strange how our inland lakes have deteriorated from the navigation of reality to the navigation of luxury. What do you see now? Motorboats! Powerboats! Speed—sailing dinghies built like dishes and used for water aquations but with no connection with sailing in the real sense. And all this in any case only a fringe that fills the lake-shore resorts, crowds round luxury hotels, and leaves the open water of Simcoe and such lakes emptier than when La Salle crossed them.

Not so in the 1880s. Navigation filled the lake.

Far out on its waters a long ribbon of smoke indicated a tug with a tow of logs heading for the mills at Jackson's Point. Sailing vessels, lumpy, heavy, and ungainly, and nearly as broad as long, carried quarry stone and heavy stuff from the top of Lake Couchiching to the railway pier at Belle Ewart. The *Emily May* steamer that circulated the lake all day and all night (in her prime days), with double crew, half of it awake and half asleep— two captains, two mates, two stewardesses, and two bartenders. The railways bit off her job point by point and place by place, the railway to Sutton and Jackson's Point being the last straw that broke her back. Yet for years after the passenger boats in the real sense had gone the excursion lived on. *Ho! for Beaverton!* read its placards on the boardside fence, *Ho! for Jackson's Point*—and then it was a summer morning carrying its sons of England, or its Knights of Ireland, its brass band, its improvised bar, its ladies' cabin as tight shut and as uncomfortable as being at home—all that went with Ho! for a day on the water in 1880. And so for years. Then came the motorcar and killed all that was left of navigation.

And all this time, although we didn't know, for my mother kept it hidden from us, at intervals my father drank, drove away to the village in the evening to return late at night after we were in bed, or lay round the farm too tired to work, and we thought it was the sun. And the more he drank, the more the farm slid sideways and downhill, and the more the cloud of debt, of unpaid bills, shadowed it over, and the deeper the shadow fell, the more he drank. My mother, I say, hid it all from us for years with a devotion that never faltered. My father, as he drank more, changed towards us from a superman and hero to a tyrant, from easy and kind to fits of brutality. I was small enough to escape from doing much of the farm chores and farm work. But I carry still the recollection of it—more, no doubt, than Jim or Dick ever did. In fact, the sight and memory of what domestic tyranny in an isolated, lonely home, beyond human help, can mean helped to set me all the more firmly in the doctrine of the rights of man and Jefferson's liberty.

By the end of the year 1881 the "old farm" as a going concern had pretty well come to a full stop. Bad farming had filled the fields with weeds; wild oats, a new curse of Ontario farming spread by the threshing machines, broke out in patches in the grain; low prices cut out all profit; apples rotted on the ground; potatoes hardly paid the digging. There was the interest of the mortgage of two hundred and fifty dollars a year, wages not paid, store bills not paid—just a welter of debt and confusion. So my father was led to give it all up and go away to Manitoba, the new land of promise that all the people on the farms were beginning to talk about. The opening of the Northwest by the Dominion taking it over had revealed the secret, so carefully guarded for two hundred years, that what had been thought of as a buffalo pasture and a fox range, a land for the trapper to share with the aurora borealis, was in reality a vast bed of deep alluvial soil, black mould two or three feet deep, the gift of the ages, the legacy of the grass and the flowers that had blossomed and withered unseen for centuries. You had but to scratch and throw in the wheat, and with that, such crops would grow as older Canada had never seen! But with that no clearing of the land to do, no stubborn fight against the stumps still all around us on the Ontario farms—empty country and land for the asking, one hundred and sixty acres free under the new homestead law and more if you wanted it "for a song." No phrase ever appealed to the farmer's heart like that of getting land for a song! In the glory of the vision he forgets that he can't sing and starts off looking for it.

To this was added the fact that there was rail connection now (1878) all the way to Manitoba by Chicago and St. Paul and the Red River route, and that it was known that the new government —which carried the election of 1878 under John A. Macdonald—was pledged to build a Canadian Pacific Railway clear across the plains and over the Rockies to the ocean. And with that was set up a sort of suction that began to draw people to Manitoba from all the Ontario farms, and presently beyond that from the old country itself, and in particular to Winnipeg, a place that had been a sort of straggled-out settlement of the Hudson's Bay Company, Fort Garry, and now broke on the horizon as a town whose geographical sight in the bottleneck entrance of the West marked it as a future metropolis. Hence the "Winnipeg boom" and the noise of hammers and the saws, and the shouts of the real-estate agents, selling real estate all day and all night, and selling it so far out on the prairie that no one ever found it again.

My father was to go to Manitoba not on his own initiative—he hadn't any—but at the call of a younger brother who had gone on ahead and was already riding on the crest of the wave. This was "my remarkable uncle," to whose memory I have devoted many sketches and even the scenario of a moving picture which I hope will one day move. He had come out to Canada, to our farm, in 1878, had captivated the countryside with his brilliant and unusual personality, taken a conspicuous part in the election of 1878, and passed on to the larger local notoriety in Toronto. He scented Winnipeg from afar, was one of the first in, and at the time of which I speak was piling up a fortune on paper, was elected to the New Manitoba legislature, and heaven knows what.

In my sketches I referred to my father and uncle

as going away together, which is an error in the record. My father, and presently my brother Jim, followed.

So we had a sale at the farm at which, as I have said elsewhere, the lean cattle and the broken machinery fetched only about enough in notes of hand (nobody had cash) to pay for the whiskey consumed at the sale.

So my father left for the West, and my mother was left on the farm with the younger children and Old Tommy, and my elder brothers and I were sent away to school at Upper Canada College. That was for me practically the end of the old farm, though the rotten place hung round our family neck for years, unsalable. For the time being it was rented to the neighbouring farmer for two hundred and fifty dollars a year, the same amount as my mother had to pay on the mortgage. The farmer didn't pay the rent and Mother didn't pay the mortgage; all debts in those days dragged along like that. But the year after that my mother moved into Toronto on the strength of a casual legacy from England that should have been hoarded as capital but was burned up as income. Then my father came back (broke) from the Northwest in 1886, and that meant another move back from Toronto to the old farm, but I was not in it, being a boarder at Upper Canada College. Things went worse than ever for my father on his return to the farm—a shadowed, tragic family life into which I need not enter. I always feel that it is out of place in an autobiography to go into such details. The situation ended by my father leaving home again in 1887. No doubt he meant to come back, but he never did. I never saw him again. My mother lived on at the old farm, because it was unsalable, for four more years, with eight children to look after as best she could on about eighty dollars a month and with Old Tommy and his wife as bodyguard. Tommy's wages had not been paid for so long that he couldn't leave, but anyway he didn't want to. In his old-fashioned Yorkshire mind wages due from the aristocracy were like shares in the National Debt. My elder brothers Jim and Dick had both left home for good, both to the West, Dick into the Northwest Mounted Police and Jim in the wake of my remarkable uncle. That made me—my father being gone—the head of the family at seventeen. But since I was away at school and college and then teaching school, I was at the farm only on holidays and odd times. I at last got rid of the rotten old place on my mother's behalf simply by moving Mother off it and letting it go to the devil —mortgages, creditors, and all. I don't know who finally got it. But for me the old farm life ended with my going to Upper Canada College in the beginning of the year 1882.

MY EDUCATION

AND WHAT I

THINK OF

IT NOW

I CAME down to Toronto from our old farm and entered Upper Canada College as a boarder in February 1882. My two elder brothers Jim and Dick had been sent on ahead (I don't remember why) the November before. So from this time on, for seventeen and a half years as a schoolboy (boarder or day), or as a student, or teacher, or as both college student and teacher together, Toronto was the city I lived in and has retained all the detail of remembrance and the peculiar charm of the past which goes with one's own city. Nor did I see any other, anyway, for about ten years.

Toronto was then just in its final stage of comfortable and completed growth as a prominent centre of life and industry, intercourse and arts, before the coming of the electrical age brought the rapid transit and communication that was to turn it into something ten times greater; to foster suburban growth, bring great industries to the fringe of the city itself, feed the country in part from the city as its base, and turn all such provincial towns into metropolitan centres. Toronto today, we admit, is ten times the size it was then. Yet perhaps in a certain aspect the advantage is not all with the new as against the old. Individual life, now lost in the mass, perhaps felt larger.

I have written a description of the Toronto of those earlier days in a book of mine on Canada, which was distributed as a private gift book and did not reach the hands of the public and from which therefore I may fittingly quote in these pages:

"In Upper Canada, henceforth Ontario, Toronto was a commodious capital city of 60,000 inhabitants. Its streets were embowered in leaves above which rose the many spires of the churches. Its wooden slum district was herded into the centre and, like poverty itself, forgotten. Where the leaves ended a sort of park land began and in it stood the University of Toronto, secular and scientific, but housed in Norman architecture of beauty unsurpassed. To the west, more rural but less beautiful with earthly beauty, was Trinity College, founded in protest against the existence of secular Toronto. But down below, along the water front, was a business district, built like a bit of London, all of a skyline and with cobblestones rattling with cabs. The new railways sliced off, as everywhere in Ontario, the shore line, vilified with ash heaps and refuse. All over Canada, between the vanishing beauty of nature and the later beauty of civic adornment, there extended this belt of tin cans and litter.

"Just above the railway lines rose the red brick Parliament buildings, the red brick Government House flew its flag, and over the way the red brick Upper Canada College set itself to make scholars and gentlemen as good as real ones. Guarding the harbour entrance was the Old Fort, its frame barracks of the same old pattern and roof slope that had already gone round the Empire, its ramparts crumbling but its ponderous old guns in embrasures still looking feebly dangerous. The tone of society was English at the top, but the barbershops spoke American. There was profound peace and order, and on Sunday all bells and Sunday-best. It seems, as most places do, a pleasant place in retrospect. At least it was cheap. The chair at Toronto that Professor Huxley tried in vain to get carried a salary of £400 and meant an ample living.

"From the business district the shops ran for half a mile up Yonge Street and, beyond that, Yonge Street ran thirty-five miles to Holland Landing where water communication began. It had a tavern to every mile and plenty of grain wagons to keep them busy. The main railway ran through from Montreal to Sarnia-Chicago. But from the half dozen little railway stations of the Toronto of early Confederation days, there radiated, like the fingers of a hand, half a dozen little railways with various gauges, reaching out north to the lumber woods—Huntsville, Coboconk, Haliburton—and north and west to the lake ports of Lake Huron and the Georgian Bay. Along the stations of these railway lines the horse and buggy and the lumber wagon took up the traffic. General stores, each a post office, with a near-by blacksmith shop, arose at the crossroads, and if there was also a river with a waterfall, there appeared a sawmill and a gristmill, and presently, as the farms multiplied, a village. Then the village became a little town, with not one but rival stores, a drugstore, a local paper, and a cricket club. In it were four churches and three taverns. One church was of the Church of England, one Presbyterian, while the Roman Catholics, Methodists, and Baptists divided the other two. On the map of Ontario, Protestantism was everywhere, but Roman Catholicism ran in zigzags. The three taverns were one Grit, and one Tory, and one neither. Many things in Ontario ran like that in threes, with the post office and the mail stage alternating as the prize of victory in elections. The cricket club is now just a memory, gone long ago. Thus the little Ontario town grew till the maples planted in its streets overtopped it and it fell asleep and grew no more. It is strange this, and peculiar to our country, the aspect of a town grown from infancy to old age within a human lifetime."

Upper Canada College, to describe it more narrowly, occupied all the space lying along King Street and extending from Simcoe Street to John Street and backward to Adelaide Street. I have no idea how many acres this meant, but there seemed lots of it: room for spacious gardens and big chestnut trees and such in front, the school building, a large square red brick structure of three stories with ample windows, occupying the centre and flanked right and left with the masters' houses (square, separate, comfortable houses, with one at the left end of the row of buildings more commodious and with a large fenced-in garden beside it which constituted the principal's residence). Some of the boys at that time were housed in masters' houses, but the bulk of them were in a building that stood farther still to the left—the Boardinghouse, red brick, two stories high, shaped like the letter T, but with much more crosspiece to the T than the upright. One end of the crosspiece was the Old Wing, made up of rooms each holding four boys—the Nurseries, they called them. The other end, still called the New Wing and only about ten years old, was cut into rooms holding two boys each. In the Old Wing there lived two resident masters with the boys, one on each floor. Each had a comfortable sitting room and a bedroom and the services of a waiter to serve his evening supper. These, of course, were junior unmarried masters with position adequate and comfortable to that status. It had grown to be the custom that young men held this position after graduation in arts and studied medicine while active as resident masters. A number of men who were later among the distinguished medical men of Ontario served this apprenticeship to aid them in their medical course.

The senior boys lived in the New Wing under the care of the senior resident master, who occupied a permanent position, had a suite of rooms, a waiter of his own, and lived in what seemed to us, as schoolboys, magnificent luxury. This was the position held for a whole generation by "Gentle" John Marland, M.A., Oxon., famous in the history of the school. The upright of the T was filled with a large dining room and, over it, a large night study. There was a smaller dining room across the far end of the New Wing, but it was used only for midday dinner, when a certain number of day boys took their dinner at school and the space in the main dining room was insufficient. All the boys from the Nurseries went into night study from seven to nine (I think it was), but the senior boys studied in their rooms.

Boys were not allowed to leave the school grounds except on Saturday and Sunday, but there was a little tuckshop called The Taffy on the street behind the school (Adelaide Street) to which leave was given every afternoon. The boys went over half a dozen at a time, for twenty minutes, according to lists drawn up by the drill sergeant. One could do oneself very well with five cents a trip—three cents for pop drink out of the bottle and two cents for two doughnuts or cakes or such things.

The school at that time was at the height of its reputation and popularity. There were very few private schools of any size in the province except the once-famous school of Dr. Tassie in Galt, and the only "rival" school in a real sense was Trinity College School, Port Hope. This had been founded, in the interest of the Church of England, with a special view to educating the sons of its clergy and the sons of members of the church who distrusted the "godlessness" that they saw spreading over education in Toronto. All who know the city will recall its long story of friction as between various degrees of godliness and god-lessness. Governor Simcoe and his aristocratic set-tlement at Muddy York were all for the Church of England. But the members of the Church of Scotland and the Scottish churches couldn't be ignored; nor, presently, the Methodists and the Baptists. Hence it was hard to find a way, even if one granted full freedom of worship, of reconcil-ing the claims of the different Protestant sects and varieties. This applied especially to the division of the vast area of public land (one eighth of it) originally set aside, when the province was created (1791), for the support of the Protestant clergy.

The difficulty applied also to all creation of public education, notably that of a university. Make it a part of the Church of England and half the prov-ince would be against it. Make it suit all the Prot-estants at once and you got it so broad that to the true churchman it appeared flat, trampled to the ground. Thus it was that when the provincial uni-versity was at last put on a wide basis as the Univer-

sity of Toronto, a seceding body headed by the
vigorous Bishop Strachan, heir to the Simcoe tradition, founded Trinity University. Upper Canada
College, all through its early years, in fact till 1891,
was financially, and by its endowments, united
with the University of Toronto. Hence came the
formation of Trinity College School, Port Hope,
to offset this connection with ungodliness. It was
at the time the only rival. Ridley College (separat-
ing low-church godlessness from high-church godliness) came later, as did also St. Andrews, separat-
ing I forget what from what, except perhaps the
crude ugliness of the Upper Canada College of
1891 from its own rural beauty—a school built by
people who knew what a school was as compared
with people who just took a guess—starting from
a deaf-and-dumb asylum or a penitentiary.

So the school on King Street was, I say, at the
height of its reputation and prosperity in 1882.
There were about one hundred boarders and over
one hundred day boys, but of course the boarders

were, and thought themselves, the school. They had never introduced the division of play hours and work hours specially adapted for Warden, as in British schools, with playtime in the best of the afternoon and school and study time in the worst. School ended at three, and all the day boys went home and the boarders had the afternoon to play till teatime. But this division was not specially made for the sake of the day boys but by the custom of the country. People forget anyway that darkness falls on autumn and winter playgrounds far earlier in Great Britain than in the more southerly latitude of Toronto.

The old school, as I see it, was a fine, decent place, with no great moral parade about it, no moral hypocrisy, but a fundamental background of decent tradition. I have elsewhere described what I have called the struggle of the school to make us gentlemen—or even Christian gentlemen —with the conclusion that it couldn't be done. We always looked on it as a false hope ourselves. I think it must have been Dr. Arnold of Rugby who first said that it didn't matter whether the school was a school of one hundred boys or of one boy but it must be a school of Christian gentlemen. Since then all headmasters of boarding schools have made that announcement in the Assembly Hall, but they fail to put it over. Certainly it failed with us at Upper Canada: we knew it was well meant but outside the realm of practical life. But the moral tone was good. There was little, indeed none, of that hideous bullying which has been the curse of many English schools; nothing, that I ever saw or knew about, of that brutal beating, flogging of boys by masters just one layer short of criminal insanity. There was none of the "fagging" of little boys as servants for the seniors, in which many British people seem to exult as a rare feature of school life but which I personally have never been able to understand. Church and religious service there was, but not too much of it, and the little there was was formal and impersonal. We had Sunday school each Sunday morning, consisting (for Church of England boys) of reciting the collect for the day. But by the time the master had read an opening prayer and heard all the collects, then, I think, Sunday was "all" and he read a benediction. All boys went to church, according to their parents' preferences. The Church of England boys, the majority, needed two churches—St. George's near by, up John Street, and the Cathedral along King Street. There was a master in charge, but they didn't go in a flock. Presbyterians went to St. Andrew's and Methodists went somewhere else. Among all the wonders there were only three or four Roman Catholics.

But the morality of the school lay in the ideas that guided it, being, of course, the ideas of decent families from which we came. We didn't lie, except in the sort of neutral zone where lying didn't count, such as in making up a list for leave to go to The Taffy (the tuckshop). There was no stealing and indeed very little to steal. Pocket money was recommended as twenty-five cents a week for junior boys, fifty cents for seniors. The era of "new rich," of schoolboy luxury, of ostentatious parents, had not yet come.

It has been a singularly fortunate thing for Canada that the foundation of Upper Canada College, and presently of other private schools on the same plan, has never created any disturbing division of education by a crosswise division of social classes such as vexes England now. As everybody knows, the problem of the "public" schools (Eton, Harrow, Rugby, and one hundred less-known others, apparently called public schools because that is the last word that any stretch of language could apply to them) rises on the horizon as one of the great postwar problems of England. Till yesterday, as it were, in spite of the successive advances of political rights, nominal political equality, England remained a country profoundly based on class and accepting it. Landed property, hereditary rights, social class, and the privileges and posts of government held in accordance with it, was the real basis of British Administration in spite of all the expansion of legal rights from the Reform Act of 1832 and onwards.

The public schools of England were a part of it, had grown up as a part of it, and can be thought of only in that light. Generations of people, not rich, but adhering to the class, gentlemen with a grip all the tighter for the forces tugging it away, clung to the idea of sending their boys to a public school, no matter what the sacrifice—a public

school, the old school tie—and then off, if need be,
for British Columbia or Matabeleland. There was
often much in it that meant out of sight out of
mind. Parents in an English rectory who said that
"Jack was doing well in Manitoba" would have felt
less sure of it if they could have seen Jack sleeping
in straw as the ostler of a livery stable. But for
others a little higher up or more fortunately connected, the "public schools" and the school tie presently meant the civil service, the foreign office, the
vast administrative range reserved, not by law but
by practice, for gentlemen.

All this is breaking up in England in the new
world now shaping. All the wealth of the old
hereditary classes available for endowed schools
and pious foundations is just nothing as beside
the national fund of public money available for
buildings, apparatus, and equipment, et cetera, of
public schools in the real sense. The lean kine have
eaten up the fat. The penny-a-week national school
of my Porchester days has grown to the vast science
college of today, based on the people's money and
itself only a part, co-operating and competing with

the state education of America and the outside world.

What then are they to do? Just have one set of schools in England, all maintained by the State? But if so, asks the country rector and the retired colonel, are you sure that you would turn out gentlemen? Leave it all alone to the open competition of pounds, shillings, and pence, people paying for what they want different from a state school or else going without it? But in that case few public schools could survive—Eton and Harrow and such, but the bulk, not. Certainly they could not survive if they tried to adapt their education to the new demands of practical science, engineering, aeronautics, without which any school is left behind mumbling Greek. The "classics" held their place as the equipment for a ruling class. That is all over. No class can rule that can't understand the science that holds in its hands the life and death of the world.

Such is the English public-school problem, an included part of the problem of a classless society. Luckily for us, the problem is not ours. Give our people cash money enough and they will take a chance on what class you class them in.

So, as we say, it was a good thing that the foundation of Upper Canada College and its fellow private schools did not create a line of class division running through the schools of the province, as between schools for gentlemen and schools for other people. The reason lay in the difference of circumstance as between Upper Canada and England. In Upper Canada, from the days of the Loyalists on, all the sensible people were advocates of schools. Those who came from Massachusetts and New York knew what they had left behind, as did those who migrated from Scotland. Hence there grew up in the province an excellent system of public elementary and presently public high schools, and they got better and better as time went on, and then the high schools in the larger towns took on more equipment and a bigger staff and turned into collegiate institutes. As against this, in England, there was no public elementary education worthy of the name till the Act of 1870, and even after the system was set up by the fact that in the eyes of most people a board school was no place for a gentleman's son.

But in Canada, gentlemen or not, people, even well-to-do people, living in the big towns mostly saw no reason why they shouldn't send their sons to high school, where the teaching was excellent and the companionship corresponded pretty much to what they got themselves in their social life. The thing was true also the other way round. Many of the boys sent to Upper Canada were not sent there because they were specially rich or specially gentlemanly, but because, as in the case of my brothers and myself, they lived in out-of-the-way places and there was nothing else to do with them.

All this got truer and truer as time went on, as education became less and less classical, as science made greater and greater demands on public money for premises and apparatus. Then came the Great War, and the splendid record of boys from high-school and collegiate existence obliterated any surviving notion of the private schools as the home of an officer class. The case of the Royal Military College at Kingston, founded in 1876, stands by itself. It was, and is, a technical school devoted single-mindedly to the profession, with an *esprit de corps* and a pride of its own that in no way interferes with other affiliations and affections.

So then there remains only the question, Is a boarding school any good anyway, except for boys whose homes are isolated from day schools? Is there anything of value in the life and experience of a boarding school that a boy cannot get in a day school? It is a question that has been put to me hundreds of times. And I think that within proper limitations and understanding the answer is in favour of the boarding school. I say limitations and understandings. For I would never agree with the British people of the older type who think a boarding school (one made for gentlemen) so necessary that they would take a chance on sending their sons to a bad one than not to any at all. The harm of a bad boarding school, an immoral place, out-weighs one hundred times all the shortcomings (after all only negative) of a day school. Parents should never send their boys to a boarding school unless they are assured of it on the side of a decent moral life. A rotten school does harm that nothing can ever remedy. So also, in a less vital sense, does a snobbish school, one whose aim is to take in money (from those who can pay it in potsful) and turn out gentlemen—as far as boys can be made so by expensive clothes, expensive habits, premature luxury, and exotic accents.

Leaving out the rotten schools and the snobbish schools, the decent boarding school has certain disciplines in life to offer, salutary and useful, not to be got elsewhere. One is the value of the break from home, of being compelled for the first time to stand on one's own feet. It is in choking down the sobs of homesickness that we first learn how much home has meant, and how fond we are of it, and the humbler and more dilapidated the home, the more suffocating is the sob of affection for it. With the break from home we learn a whole lot of new values—as, for instance, that of the friend in need, the decent fellow who shows the new boy where everything is and where to put things away: first thing you know, you are talking to him about your home and how your mother had warned you not to pack your books the wrong way into your trunk, and he says that about half his stuff got bashed up on the train coming down, and so there you are two fellow adventurers, both smashed up by railway baggagemen. How eagerly a new boy at school reaches out for such contacts of friendliness, like the shoots of a young plant on hard ground; how quickly he responds to a kind accent in a master's tone, to a hand upon his shoulder; with what penetration he sees that the old drill sergeant, even if half tipsy, isn't half bad, and what encouragement he finds in a half wink and a "cheer up" from the jolly old janitor. Then, as the days go by and the weeks go by, and he begins to settle into the place and have his part in it, what a new life and pride—something about him, as it were, that is his, that he has made, a new integument about him like the shell put on by a crab.

It is this new integument—call it, if you like, this new fellowship—that gives the peculiar meaning to boarding-school friendship, even as the years go by and it all turns into retrospect, to broadening companionship and acquaintance. It is a commonplace, as often repeated as it is true, that the friend-

ships made at boarding school are different in
kind, deeper in meaning, than ordinary friendships.
And how they last. I am not thinking here of the
school friendships of men who were at school together and, to the good luck of circumstances, spent
their life side by side. I am thinking rather of those
who were boys together at school and for uncounted
years, for long decades, never saw one another, life
passing separately for each of them, yet bring them
casually together after twenty years, after forty if
you like, and the passage of the years is just as
nothing, the call of the past bridges it in an instant.

Such has often been my experience, meetings
with boys of the old school whom I had neither
seen nor much thought about for half a lifetime.
It was after one of my lectures in a great American
city, a lecture to be followed by a reception, that
they told me that there would be a Mr. Lyon at the
reception who told them that he had been at Upper
Canada College with me fifty years before. Did I
remember him? Remember him? What a ridiculous
question, remember Eph Lyon, three years senior
to me, one of the stars of the First (Cricket)
Eleven: a big, striking fellow—as a boy I put him

at over six feet, say six and a half—in a cricket blazer, walking back from the wickets to the marquee scoring tent at the corner of the college cricket ground, amid the burst of applause that greeted his score of thirty not out? And I, a college junior, not even fit for the Third Eleven. Remember him? No, the only thing was the compliment that he remembered me.

So there he was, sure enough, in the crush of the reception, one of those stand-up-and-talk affairs where one lady was asking me what I thought of Galsworthy's *White Monkey* (I hadn't heard of it) and another telling me that I ought to have gone on lecturing another half hour. But for me Lyon was the feature of the reception. I admit that fifty years had altered him. He had turned from a Canadian schoolboy into an American businessman. He had lost about a foot in height and most of his width. He said the lecture was fine and that he never came to them, and then he asked me what became of Old Gentle, and I told him that all the old school buildings had been knocked down and the ground remade and rebuilt into great square blocks, and we stood there in the dust and memory of the falling schoolhouse, the wind from the chestnut trees of the college garden blowing in our faces. All about us was the babble of Galsworthy's *White Monkey* and literary discussion, but the call of the years had carried us beyond it.

Or, similarly, I recall how one day at my club a message came to me to say that a gentleman from Arizona was downstairs in the lower hall who said he had been at school with me fifty years ago. I went down, and there he was, sure enough. Who would he be? Why, Jimmy Douglas, of course. Who else could he be, though I hadn't seen him? We were in Form 2A together and in the old boardinghouse together in 1882. "Well, Jimmy!" I said as I asked him whether he remembered that he had said to me in 2A that he believed a fellow didn't need algebra. Evidently he hadn't needed it in Arizona, solid and prosperous, rugged and simple without it, and, as memory cleared away the haze from his features, unchanged since twelve years ago.

Another time, in my club also, a man said, "Let

me introduce my cousin," and I exclaimed as I shook hands with what looked like a tall, very dignified and formal gentleman but which I knew wasn't, but was just a schoolboy in disguise. "Why! Hullo! Friday!" He laughed. It is amazing how quickly the barriers break down. "Friday, all right," he said, "but no one has called me that for forty years." "You remember," I said, "how you entered Upper Canada College alongside of a boy from Cobourg called Crusoe, and after the master had written down Crusoe's name he said to you, 'I suppose you must be Friday'?" With that the scene rose before us, the typical master's joke, that goes such a long way with a class, the subservient laughter, and afterward, in the playground, the nickname *Friday,* plastered on and there for keeps.

All that, I say, is apropos of the question, What is there in a boarding school?—to which the answer is that there is a heap. Incidentally, though I forgot to mention it before, in my day a boarding school still carried the advantage that it gave athletics, games, and the life surrounding them. This exclusive aspect is gone in our present age, when athletics and sports are universal and the new and wholesome worship of health, strength, and fitness is a dominant idea of the day. Yet even in athletics the bond of union for the boarding school is always closer and more real.

For me my first initiation into boarding-school life and into the valley of tears of homesickness in February 1882 was brief enough. I entered at an awkward time scholaretically, though it fitted the financial quarters of the year, because all the subjects had been begun and for the moment I didn't fit in anywhere. The class in algebra had begun at New Year's, and I hadn't had any, so the master in charge said to one of the boys, "McKeown, take this boy to the back of the room and explain to him what algebra is." McKeown did so, and I don't believe that even the great Arabian scholar, Ibn Ben Swot, who invented algebra and gave it its Arabic name, could have put it more exactly where it belonged, as mystery, than did McKeown of Form 2A in 1882. McKeown set out his Todhunter's *Algebra* and some bits of paper on a desk. He opened Todhunter at a page marked Examples and all spotted with x, y, and z, mixed with figures. I had never seen algebra before. "Now," said McKeown, "you take x," and he wrote it down. "We'll say it's ten." "Is it?" I said. "Say it is," said McKeown. "Then, you see, x plus one equals eleven." "But," I persisted, "how do you know x is ten?" "I don't," said McKeown. "Say it's twelve if you like." "No, no," I said, "I only meant how much *is* x?" "Oh, I don't know," said McKeown, and of course that is exactly what Ibn Ben Swot would have said, only McKeown felt ashamed of ignorance and Ibn Ben exulted in it. Indeed he would have explained that the whole point of algebra is that it enables us to deal with unknown quantities, so much of this and so much of that, and find out all sorts of results connected with it, without giving them any single fixed meaning.

I spent three or four days in such class exercises and in standing up, utterly homesick, and chorusing out declensions and conjugations, after the old-fashioned system of the day, and in living through clattering meals that I could hardly eat for homesickness, and in night study, and in the nursery bedroom with my two brothers, and then the fourth or fifth day brought it all suddenly to a close. I woke up in the morning with a headache and my stomach was as red as a lobster, and that was scarlatina. So the lady matron of the boardinghouse took me in charge and packed up a bag of my things and said, "And now come and see what a nice little house we have out behind the school!" It didn't look to me like a nice little house; in fact it looked just like a brick coal shed converted into two rooms as a "sanatorium," which is just what it was. This was before the days of isolation hospitals and trained nurses. So there I was, established in the sanatorium under the care of an old dame, a kinder and a cleaner version of Mrs. Gamp. My illness was nothing and was over in a day, and then the next day somehow my mother turned up and I didn't care how long I stayed isolated, drawing pictures and having her read out loud to me.

At the end of so many weeks I went back to the old farm and in the intervals of convalescence went up and down to the red school twice a week, learning Latin. After Easter I went back to Upper Canada, but in less than no time it had all changed, all began to feel familiar and easy. The lessons were to me a mere nothing, because they had shoved me a class down and I knew it all, and with that I began to make a few timid friendships and to feel proud of walking with my friends down King Street all in college cricket caps (dark blue and white) and hearing people say as they passed, "Those are Upper Canada boys." Oh my! Eh what! I remember how my bygone friend Chic Sales, that great artist of the comic, told me that the first time he heard someone say in a hotel rotunda, "Look, that's Chic Sales!" he threw his head up so high with pride that he tripped his left foot behind his right and made a sort of stage fall into the air. Chic had the imitation down to perfection. That is exactly how my twelve-year-old associates and I felt when someone said, "Upper Canada boys!" Then came the springtime and the cricket season of May and June. The college grounds all beautiful, great days on Saturday afternoons, cricket matches and heroes, and receptions with great talk, ice cream and cakes, and then, ecstatic beyond wonder, the close of the term, the school breaking up in a torrent of oratory, exhorting us to be gentlemen, packing trunks, and off to take the train to go home for the holidays. My brothers and I went down to the little old Toronto and Nipissing Station at the foot of Berkeley Street two hours before the train was due to be made up and "fooled around" among the cinder head beside the bay, waiting to start home, and there wasn't a dull minute in all the two hours.

We came back as boarders that autumn, and after that, as I said before, I stayed on at Upper Canada, passing all through the school as a boarder and as a day boy and finally as a boarder again. My brother Jim dropped out to go to "my remarkable uncle" in Winnipeg, and Dick presently grew so tall that they couldn't keep him there any longer. Dick couldn't learn anything by any known academic process. They promoted him out of the first form into the second on the ground that he was nearly six feet high, but they refused to carry him beyond six feet. So Dick dropped out and back to the old farm, now occupied only by Old Tommy, the hired man. Then presently there came the Northwest Rebellion of 1885, which brought after it that autumn an outbreak of placards calling for recruits for the Northwest Mounted Police. Dick ran true to form, made his way to Ottawa, was accepted, and then off to the Regina barracks. My younger brother Charlie filled in in his place at Upper Canada as a day boy alongside of me.

I look back to the education I received in those years and I find in it plenty to think about. It was what is, or was, called a splendid classical education, as it was for a couple of hundred years, in England and America, looked on as the mainstay of national culture, the keystone in the arch of civilization; and before that in England it was the only kind of education and it was embedded deep in theology and so intimately connected with the Church that it was inseparable from it. Any form of education not connected with the Church was held to belong to the devil, as witness the education for which Oxford in its infant years imprisoned or secluded Roger Bacon for ten years. There was the Church's education and the devil's education. In the long run the devil's education has won out. Any nation whose leaders are not trained in it will no longer survive; any nation whose life is not based on it, whose people are not equipped with it, cannot last a generation. In other words, the "survival quality" that was attributed to the old classical education has passed away, or is visibly passing away, with the generation of the present leaders.

People who admit they know nothing of the history of education among English-speaking peoples may tolerate a few words of explanation. All through the Middle Ages the only education (we are speaking broadly) was that of the Church. It was carried on in Latin. When the modern age began, say about A.D. 1500, and printing multiplied books, education widened and included a lot of what had been the education of the Greek and Romans, such as the philosophy of Aristotle, which in no way contradicts the teaching of the Church and could be read side by side with it, and the great poems and plays of the Greeks, of Homer and the tragedians, and those of Rome, such as Vergil's account of how Aeneas escaped from the fall of Troy and founded the Roman nation, and the great histories, Thucydides' *History of Greece,* and the works of Livy and Tacitus and Julius Caesar in

Latin of Demosthenes and of Cicero. All this made such an imposing body of literature, especially when set off in the new glory of print on vellum, that there was in vernacular English, or indeed in any vernacular, nothing like it at all. It was so to speak the world's literature, containing all the wisdom of the world. Even when people in England such as Shakespeare began to write things that were bitter no one knew it or admitted it. Many people still don't. A Greek professor, especially if growing old and apt to sit under a tree and fall asleep over Theocritus, will tell you, of course, that Greek literature is unsurpassed. Nor can you contradict him, since you don't know it except by telling him that the Chinese classics are better still.

So here then was the education that went into the rising glory of England and with the earliest beginnings of the United States. Oddly enough it carried with it a fringe, which kept growing and expanding, of mathematics and physics that had not been part of the education of the Greeks at large. The Greeks abhorred anything practical (just as Oxford one hundred years ago tried to ignore "stinks," meaning chemistry), and they never had any decent system of calculation by numbers on paper, so that Greek mathematics was queer, odd, ingenious stuff, as if one worked out puzzles for puzzles' sake. It was complicated and difficult enough, as when they speculated on the kind of curves made by slicing through a cone (conic sections), an enquiry carried on "just for fun" in their time. Only one part of their Greek mathematics, the art of field measurement, or geometry, was especially developed into a complete and rounded form, particularly in Egypt, in the great Greek centre of learning in Alexandria. This was because in Egypt, with each annual flood of the Nile, land measurement by sight lines had a special importance. Hence the treatise of Euclid came into our education intact and stayed there till into the present century.

To what the Greeks had of mathematics, the new English classical education, as it got consolidated after, say, A.D. 1500, added all that went with the wonderful system of calculating by giving figures a "place value" (so that, for example, the figure two may mean two, or twenty, or two hundred, and so on). We are so accustomed to this that we take it for granted and no longer see how wonderful it is. The Greeks and Romans and all the ancient nations fooled round with it and got even as close to it as the method of counting of beads on strings, et cetera, but they never learned how to put it on paper and so make the figures add and subtract and multiply in our present marvellous and simple method of columns and places. It was the Hindus who worked this out, but the Arabs put the cap on it by inventing the use of the figure zero, the round O for nothing that means everything.

Luckily for English education, mathematics developed side by side with classical education not as an equal partner but as an adjacent. This was partly by the genius of the nation which tends to produce men of exception as seen in Napier, who invented logarithms, Isaac Newton, who invented calculus and went, in an effortless way, beyond all known boundaries, and Halley, who invented Isaac Newton by keeping him at work. Nor could even Halley keep him at it for good. It is odd that Newton, who lived to a great old age, was all done with science relatively early in life, pursued no more discoveries, and felt proud to be in Royal Service as the Master of the Mint.

But what made mathematics for England was its connection with navigation. When the era of colonial expansion brought England on to the seven seas, navigation by means of mathematical astronomy became the peculiar privilege and pursuit of the British. The Portuguese and the Spanish had known only the beginnings of it. Columbus was really, in spite of some tall talk on his part, quite ignorant. He merely threw a chunk of wood overboard to see how fast the ship was going. The English forged ahead. The Elizabethans "took the sun." Isaac Newton himself explained that longitude at sea could be accurately known each day at noon as soon as someone could invent a clock to keep time at sea. Even at that the admiralty prize of ten thousand pounds went begging till late in the eighteenth century. But with the use of chronometrics and sextants and the compilations of astronomical tables worked out on shore and applied at sea, and ingenious mathematical tables of logarithms to apply them with, British navigators led the world. It was the British Government that sent out

astronomers with captains to observe the transit of
Venus in the South Pacific in 1769. After which
the use of mathematics got mixed up with the
glory of Old England and Britannia ruling the
waves, and no scheme of English education was
complete without it. Not that English schools took
to it gladly. We are told (in the *Memoirs* of General Lyttelton) that even at Eton the study of
mathematics was tolerated rather than appreciated
as late as the sixties of the last century.

In all this I am not wandering from the point.
I am explaining where I got my Upper Canada
College education from; well, that's where it came
from, from the theologians and the classical scholars and Isaac Newton and the *Nautical Almanac*.

But the thing that especially consolidated the
position of the classical education of England, as
it presently did also that of America, was the discovery, by experience, that it was a great training
for leadership. This applied particularly to a nation
which had grown not democratic, but parliamen-
tary, a nation where oratory in the legislature
counted for more and more, and where forensic
oratory in free and open counts was one of the

great highways to success and political prefer-
ment.

To this was added presently the power of the
press, the value of the written word and the per-
suading paragraph, things for which the classical
education had, and still retains when most else is
gone, a commanding eminence.

Side by side with classical education, in a
position that has slowly grown from the lowest to
the highest, grew up medicine and medical education: from its earliest beginnings, in black art
and barbers' surgery with its red-and-white rags,
out of the mists of astrology and the incantations
of superstition, out of empirical remedies and old
wives' tales, till with the age of science it began to
build on definite organised truth and on knowledge gathered from the facts of dissection and the
observations of anatomy. But medicine was no part
of the education of a cultivated man, and till far
down the nineteenth century the social status of
a doctor, other than a court physician, was dubious and humiliating.

Science remained for the few, for the investi-
gators, for the Royal Society founded under

Charles II as Prince Rupert, a factor in the national advance of England second only to the Royal Navy, for people who, like Benjamin Franklin, with electricity, wanted to know. The list of the great names in science—Priestley, Faraday, Lyell, Darwin—lies outside of the orbit of academic education.

Such was the classical education. It is my opinion that the world moved it on just in time and that England especially was saved in the nineteenth century from degenerating into intellectual stagnation only by the fact that other forces in the nation, clear outside of its scholars and all that they stood for, pursued science for science's sake; promoted invention, applied it to industry and transport, and presently—by the dead weight of circumstance and opinion—thrust it into the schools and colleges.

A chief trouble with the classical scholarship was its infernal conceit. The typical classical scholar developed under encouragement into a sort of pundit. He knew it all—not part of it, all of it. What he didn't know wasn't college. The phrase was used long after by Benjamin Jowett,

Master of Balliol, but it might have been used by any of them from the days of Dr. Busby of Westminster, in the days of Charles II, down to their last octogenarian successors of yesterday. They knew it all. That is to say, they knew nothing whatever of medicine and would have roared with laughter over their own ignorance of it, with a neat Latin quotation to cap it. They knew nothing whatever of the geographical and geological globe about them, replacing it with an intimate knowledge of the Aegean Sea as of 500 B.C. They knew nothing of modern languages, regarding them as a thing for couriers or dragomen. They knew nothing of the investigations of natural science, had no vision as to where it was leading, nothing of its application to industry, nothing of industry itself, nothing of finance—in fact, looked at in a proper focus, all that they did know was nothing as compared with the vast portentous knowledge that was rising on the horizon of a changing world.

Even for literature and the drama, all that goes with the republic of letters, their point of view was turning hopelessly astray by their persistent tradition that of course Latin and Greek literature was far superior to that of our own day. To say this in A.D. 1500 was to state a plain truth. To say it in A.D. 1900 was to say pure unadulterated nonsense.

The old classical education had at least the advantage that it was hard and difficult with no royal road. It was as hard as ever a teacher liked to make it. For witness call in anyone who has studied Greek moods and tenses or tried to translate the Greek dramatists into something intelligible. In all this it was miles above a great deal of the slush and mush, which has in part replaced it, the effortless, pretentious studies of things that can't be studied at all, the vague fermentations that tend to replace stern disciplinary work when education is all paid for and free for all and popular and universal, provided that it is not made difficult.

The classical curriculum had also the advantage, to be rightly or wrongly used, that it lent itself admirably to competitive study, to examinations, to marks, to prizes, to going up and down in class. It was from that aspect that I made my Upper Canada College education even less beneficial than it need have been, accentuated its faults by utilizing its weakness. We had at Upper Canada College the system whereby each day's class consisted mainly of questions and answers, that is, either questions on homework done the night before or on something done at sight in class. The boys sat all along one side or all across the front of the room. If the master asked a boy a question and he couldn't answer it, then it was passed on, "Next! Next!" till somebody did answer. The boy who thus answered correctly moved up above the ones who had failed to answer. Theoretically, but very rarely in practice, a question might be asked of a boy at the top of the class and be passed on, "Next! Next!" with increasing excitement all the way to the bottom boy of the class, who might answer correctly and "Go up ahead" in one swoop. Hence the system had in it a certain element of sport, something of the attraction of a horse race. At least it kept the class from going to sleep and it made the class do the work and not the teacher.

It always seems to me that in a lot of the revised education of today, which quite rightly undertook to modify the severities, the rigor, the physical punishment, and the needless difficulties of the older teaching, the mistake is made in the contrary direction. Everything is made too easy. The teacher has to "sell" the subject to the class, and in trying to make everything clear and simple it is forgotten that there are some things that can't be made clear and simple because they are by nature difficult and complex.

For me the old-fashioned system of going up and down and trying to move up to the head of the class and stay there proved altogether too congenial and attractive and helped to give a false bias to my education. In the junior form, the first and second, I took my studies easily, didn't bother whether I went up or down, and got a very good place without trying for it. But from the third form on, I got more and more drawn into study and over-study till presently I filled all my time outside of school as well as in. After the third form, by this continuous industry, I ranked first in everything except mathematics, and after the fourth form first in everything by learning by heart in mathematics every possible thing that would let itself be learned by heart.

Study by this pattern knocked all the reality out of certain subjects. History for me just turned into an underlined book of which I knew by heart all the underlined tags, headings, and dates. I knew them then and I still know all the clauses of the Treaty of Utrecht of 1713, and all sorts of dates and lists, and all kinds of headings. The reality of history gradually was lost from sight behind this apparatus of preparation for examinations.

The very thoroughness of the old classical system made it still worse suited for modern education.

TEACHING SCHOOL

I SPENT ten and a half years of my life (February 1889–July 1899) in teaching school, and I liked the last day of it as little as I liked the first. As a consequence I have spoken and written very often and very bitterly about schoolteaching and the lot of the schoolteacher. Looking back on it all, I think I ought to retract about one half of all I said, for I think now that one half of the fault was with me and only one half with the profession as such. Even at that, it seems to me a shame that schoolteaching cannot be organised as a profession which a person can enter as a lifework and in which success should bring at least the main part of what success means in the other learned professions such as medicine, law, and the church. As it is, schoolteaching offers too much at the beginning, too little as the years go

by. The initial salary is better than what anyone
could hope to gain in his opening years at law or
medicine. The final salary is nowhere beside the
great prizes the other professions offer. It is true
that in the other professions they may fall by the
way, lawyers without a case and medical men
forced out of their profession by lack of opportunity
and glad to earn a living in any other kind of way.
In teaching very few fall by the way; very many
rise out of it; but those who remain in it for a
lifetime find, as the years go on, that it gives them
less than what is fair, less than what is commen-
surate with other pursuits.

There are certain things without which the life
of a person who has grown up in cultured sur-
roundings and received a cultivated education is
not properly complete, does not stand on a fair
level with other lives and opportunities. Every
career should look forward to marriage as a thing
that can in due course and time be accepted, with
all that it brings in the way of children and a
home, without a pinch and a semi-poverty that
reduces it to a status not good enough to rank with

that of other professions. With marriage should go a sufficient command of money to allow for the amenities of life, to permit one to belong to a club, to buy, within reason, books, et cetera, furniture and house things, to enjoy art and the theatre and such special holiday "blowouts" as punctuate the monotony of life's routine. Most necessary of all is money enough to launch one's children in the world.

Any man who has that much need ask for no more. Granted that much of ease and affluence, the rest depends on himself, on what kind of mind and personality he has. The trouble with our school-teaching in Canada is that up to now it does not offer these things. Hence its characteristic features—too much at first, too little later. An in-and-out profession through which a series of bright young men pass on to something better, and in which a certain number of young men, too dull or too devoted, remain forever. The running stream leaves its deposit as it flows on, but is the deposit gold or mud?

In my case I went into schoolteaching with my eyes wide open, as into something temporary on the way to a real career. To go into teaching was a matter of sheer necessity. My education had fitted me for nothing except to pass it on to other people. And as I have explained, my mother's finances had come to a full stop with the final exertion of getting enough money to give the one year of full under-graduate status at the university for which my scholarship of one hundred dollars was quite in-adequate. Meantime, as my father had vanished into space, my mother was still on the old farm with eight children younger than I to look after and with an income of, I think, eighty dollars a month to do it on. Of my two elder brothers, Jim was in Winni-peg with some small job in the courthouse, but quite unable to send money home, and Dick in the Northwest Mounted Police had nothing to spare from his pay. How my mother managed in the en-suing years before any of us could help her I do not know. I imagine the answer is that she drifted into debt and stayed there. Even when we could pres-ently give her money it was merely applied over the surface of the debt below like a warm growth

of Arctic flowers in the sun over cold frozen mus-
keg.

I found out, by asking those who knew, that
my college status as a third-year undergraduate—
for I had taken the first and second years in one,
as already explained—would entitle me to teach
in a high school or collegiate institute, provided
I put in three months as a teacher in training. This
new feature was still quite recent, as was the first
instalment of that qualification in "education" (so
called) superadded to the academic qualification
of time spent and examinations passed at the university. From the modest three months of technical
education as a qualification for teaching, the requirement has now been lengthened in Ontario,
as it has in most similar jurisdictions in Canada
and the United States, to one year. It thus represents as much as 25 per cent of the academic qualification itself. I have always thought, and still
think, this is out of all proportion. I have always
had a very low opinion of the educational qualification—too low, I am sure—always looked upon it
as about 10 per cent solid value and 90 per cent

mixed humbug and wind. I have always felt that
the only way to learn to teach is to go and do it, just
as Mr. Squeers, immortalized by Dickens, taught
his pupils to spell *windows* by going and cleaning
them. In so far as the educational qualification
helps to close the profession and keep out super-
fluous numbers, I am convinced that the same time
and money spent on an extra academic year would
be more to the point.

I sent in my application and was duly assigned
in September of 1888 as one of a group of half
a dozen men and women teachers allotted for three
months' training to the Strathroy Collegiate Institute, Strathroy being in western Ontario, beyond
London.

So in due course I got on the train and went
to Strathroy. Apart from trips up and down to
Sutton, it was my first railway journey. I had a
wooden trunk tied with a clothesline and something called a valise—I forget whether of imitation
straw or of imitation something else. It is the kind
of baggage I still use. I have never risen to the

luxury of aristocratic baggage as a mark of status. For years I was too poor to buy it, and when I could I didn't any longer care for it. I think that Dr. Johnson once said something like that in a letter to the Earl of Chesterfield, about having a literary position. I feel just as he did about having a pigskin valise: "Had it been early it had been kind, but now I am known and do not need it." If it is true that a man is known, as is indicated in romantic novels, by his baggage, then my valise places me every time.

So, as I say, I arrived at Strathroy. I left my trunk at the station and walked up the street, and presently I saw a sign, ROOMS WITH BOARD, and went in and took a room with board. I think the price was three a week. I went upstairs and unpacked my valise and wrote a letter home and said, "Dear Mother, I arrived at Strathroy all right, but the boardinghouse I am in looks a pretty rotten place, so I don't expect to stay long." Then I went down to supper, and after I had finished it I met the landlady coming downstairs and she said, "If you find this boardinghouse such a rotten place I guess you better not stay in it," so I was on the

street again, less twenty-five cents, moving on to
the next sign ROOMS WITH BOARD.

That was the beginning of my contact with
boardinghouses, which spread intermittently over
many years and from which presently I found
much food for reflection. Some readers may recall
my *Boarding House Geometry,* in which was laid
down the axiom that all *Boarding Houses are the
same Boarding House* and the postulate that a *bee
line* may be made *from any one boarding house to
any other boarding house.* No doubt the origin of
those truths reaches back as far as Strathroy.

When I duly found a boardinghouse (across the
lapse of years I quite forget it and where it was),
and had entered the Teachers School next day,
I found it all very simple and easy beyond words
after the hard study to which I was habituated.
The little group of teachers in training moved
about the school, listened to sample lessons (in no
wise different from the lessons and classes we had
all taken for years), and presently were entitled to
stand up and "take the class" themselves under the
supervision of the teacher.

In doing this I learned on the side a lesson on

how not to be funny, or the misuse of a sense of humour which lasted me all my life and echoed back to me in a strange way nearly thirty years later. The principal of the Strathroy Collegiate was Mr. James Wetherell, the well-beloved "Jimmy" Wetherell whose memory is still dear to the heart of a thousand pupils. He seemed to us old at the time, as all adult people do to the eyes of eighteen, but he must have been relatively young, for he lived on and on, passed the opening century, still in harness when the Great War came, and died at a ripe age later on. He was a fine scholar, his chief subject, at least the one he liked best to teach, being English. But he had acquired, as most scholars do if absorbed in their work and exulting in the exposition of it, little tricks of speech and manner all his own and all too easy to imitate. I had at that time a certain natural gift of mimicry, could easily hit off people's voices and instinctively reproduce their gestures. So when Jimmy Wetherell, halfway through a lesson in English, said to me most courteously, "Now will you take the lesson over at that point and continue it?" I did so with a completeness and resemblance to Jimmy's voice and manner which of course delighted the class. Titters ran through the room. Encouraged as an artist, I laid it on too thick. The kindly principal saw it himself and flushed pink. When I finished he said quietly, "I am afraid I admire your brains more than your manners." The words cut me to the quick. I felt them to be so true and yet so completely without malice. For I had no real "nerve," no real "gall." It was the art of imitation that appealed to me. I had not realized how it might affect the person concerned. I learned with it my first lesson in the need for human kindliness as an element in humour.

Now when this happened there was in the class, somewhere on a back bench, a boy of thirteen whose name was Arthur Currie who had entered the school that autumn. He was destined to become one of the celebrated men of our Canadian Dominion, Arthur Currie, later on General Sir Arthur Currie, Commander-in-Chief of the Canadian Overseas Forces of the Great War, the victor of Vimy Ridge, a really great man. I had occasion to know it, as I served under him for the thirteen years during which he was principal of McGill. I used in those years, in public speeches, to refer to the parallel fact that Aristotle had taught Alexander the Great of Greece, and to say that in my opinion Aristotle had nothing on me. And since like all other speakers I prefer an old joke to a new, I worked this one overtime for thirteen years.

As a matter of fact, I didn't know General Currie as a boy at Strathroy School, but, with his usual and phenomenal memory, he recalled me. When he came to McGill I went, as in duty bound, to pay my respects to him in his office, and I said, for I had just been reading, as had everybody, his full biography in the newspapers, "I think, General Currie, I must have had the honour of teaching you when I was a teacher in training at Strathroy in 1888." He gave me a closer and more scrutinizing look. "Why, yes," he said, "I recognize you now; you were the young man to whom Jimmy Wetherell, the principal, said that he admired your brains more than your manners."

The work of the teachers-in-training course was easy and agreeable and companionable. Hard it was certainly not, and it was useful, provided that the quantity was kept down to the proportions then existing and not extended out of all reason, as I think it to be today. As examination work we had to study two or three books, one on school management, with discussion of such things as ventilation, et cetera, and one on the outline of the history of education. This last was very interesting, but a little of it went a long way. I should think that any trained student could get all that he needed of the history of education in a week of reading, I mean as far as its utility in actual teaching goes. Beyond that he could study it till he was grey with increasing interest to himself. The trouble with so many of our new curriculum subjects is that they confuse what is agreeable reading for old men with what is necessary reading for young ones. As I see it, the whole of sociology lies in this field, a wonderful subject of reflection for riper years but hopelessly artificial as a class study for youth.

The training school ended with examinations,

a school entertainment, and good-bye and good will all round. I found myself a qualified secondary-school teacher of the province of Ontario and a specialist in Latin, Greek, French, German, and English. I presume that I still am.

Being a specialist is one thing, getting a job is another. So I found myself back at the old farm with nothing to do but send in applications for such teaching jobs as I could hear of or find advertised in the papers. Among other things, I had the honour of being an applicant for a job on the staff of the newly founded and not yet opened Bishop Ridley College, at St. Catherine's, a school that has since traced a long and honourable record of over half a century. I doubt very much whether my application, to use an upstate expression, caused any headache to the trustees, seeing that my application for the position of modern-language master went in alongside of that of H. J. Cody, the successful applicant who had just taken his degree in arts that year. Cody had had a phenomenal record universally first in everything, so that in his year the lists in all the languages, as in English and history, began (1)

H. J. Cody, and should have added, And the
rest nowhere. He began here that long and distinguished life of service to the Church and to
education which sees him now as president of the
University of Toronto. I remember, by the way,
when we, his college contemporaries, heard that
Cody had gone into the Church, we looked on it
as a case of a good man gone astray. We realised
the success he was thus renouncing as a great
criminal lawyer or criminal politician, for his college eminence was so outstanding that he could
easily have reached out for any of the great prizes
of life. There was no other way for any college
contemporary to escape competing against Cody
except to take a dive clear into another faculty,
and even at that he would be apt in medicine to
come up alongside the similar record of Lewellys
F. Barker, later on the famous Dr. Barker of
Baltimore, who was always first in every class in
each subject. I remember that years later I asked
Barker if this was literally true and he told me
that there had been an exception, that once he
had been put into third class, and that in the very
subject which he regarded as his best and on

which he had written voluminous examination answers, all, he was certain, correct. Barker told me further that very soon after the occurrence, when he had come to know the examiner in question as a fellow doctor and fellow examiner, he asked him if he recalled how and why the third class happened. "Most certainly," answered the examiner. "I put you in third class because I wanted *answers* not a whole damn book." Those who know the vagaries of examiners will realise the truth of the story. Barker carried the bitterness of it throughout the years and never forgave the injustice. He was fond of telling the story, and at his death it appeared in many of the notices written of his career.

Meanwhile I was trying in vain in January 1889 to get a job in a school. Unexpectedly I got one at the beginning of February through the good offices of an old friend, the "Mr. Park" who had been for some years our tutor on the old farm. Park, after his tutorship ended in 1881, had gone back to college, finished his course in arts, and had gone into teaching and at this time occupied the position of headmaster of Uxbridge High

School. He wrote to me to say that a modern-language teacher was needed at the school and if I applied for the post he didn't doubt that his recommendation would get it for me. This turned out to be true, and in due course I drove over to Uxbridge and found myself installed as teacher of modern languages in the bright new red brick high school that had recently been added to the town's attractions.

Uxbridge was then a town of about fifteen hundred people, situated nowhere in particular on the high ground between Lake Ontario and Lake Simcoe, one of those agricultural centres that grew up around a gristmill and a sawmill when the settlers moved in, grew to a certain extent, and then planted trees in the street to replace the shattered forests and fell asleep under the trees. Uxbridge, as its name shows and as the adjacent township of Brock indicates, belongs among the settlements that followed the Great War (once so called) when the Battle of Waterloo and Lord Uxbridge as a Waterloo hero and General Brock's heroic death at Queenstown Heights were memories of yesterday. Around the town was settled a fine class of British people, and as beside my village of Sutton, its main street, with a flood of light from the shop-windows, looked quite metropolitan. It had the usual equipment of taverns and churches but was a clean, bright, orderly little place, dull as ditch-water but quite unaware of the fact.

From the old farm to Uxbridge was a distance of eighteen miles. Today, travelling in a motorcar over gravelled roads, there is hardly time to get well settled down in the car in a trip for such a dis-tance. But in 1889 it was a real pilgrimage, not to be done there-and-back in a day, up and down over one sand hill after another, in winter through hill cuttings blocked with snow, in spring among sunken roads covered with spring floods. Now-adays, of course, all such distances have shrunk to nothing; Toronto Sunday trippers ran out to and beyond Uxbridge to fish in the streams or drive through Uxbridge (apart from the Main Street) itself without noticing that it is there. Such as it was, the town became my home for the next half year, and I owe it all the gratitude that goes with the payment of a first salary.

I had no trouble with teaching from the very

start, no difficulty in doing it, no question of discipline. There are certain people who from the moment they step into a classroom present themselves
as easy marks to pupils inclined to disorder, who
even provoke disorder among pupils inclined to
silence and attention. I remember such among
those who taught me at Upper Canada College
as does everyone else among those who taught him
at his school. Very generally the recollection of
such incompetents is among the fondest memories
retained across the years. Pupils or students look
back to the memory of "old Billy," or whoever it
was who couldn't keep order, with a singular gratitude, with a laughing memory that is all attention.
Such incompetents cannot be trained out of it.
They are hopeless from the start. I remember (years
later than Uxbridge) how General Currie at Mc-
Gill undertook to explain the principles of class
discipline to a young, incompetent teacher at-
tached to my department whose students were
turning his classroom into a bear garden. "Mr.
Smith," said the general, "you can't keep order.
Now listen, you were a soldier in my army, weren't
you?" "Yes sir." "In France, weren't you?" "Yes

sir." "Well, then, can't you take the first of these miserable young—— (General Currie here used his own private vocabulary) who starts trouble in the class out on the campus and try to kill him?" "Yes sir," said Mr. Smith. Yet within another month or so the class had Mr. Smith beaten to a standstill. He had to give up teaching and was out in a cruel world without resources. I have often wondered what would have happened if Mr. Smith had murdered a McGill student on the campus. But no doubt General Currie was right. The mere intent to murder, the murderous look, was all that was needed. Poor Smith couldn't command it.

At Uxbridge I didn't have to murder or threaten to murder any of my pupils. Instinctively I went at class order in the right way, and when you know how, it is very simple. It is the beginning which counts. Face the class. Begin talking to them at once. Get to business, not with one of them but with all of them. Talk: don't mumble. Face them: don't turn your back. Start work: don't get fumbling about with a class list of names and a roll call, which you may pronounce correctly or may not. Leave all that till later. Start work, and, once started, they are lost as far as disorder goes. In fact they won't expect any. Above all, don't try to be funny; feeble teachers attempt a footing of fun as a means of getting together. The real teacher descends to fun only when he has established a sufficient height to descend from.

So there I was with my class, all bright and easy with Pass Matriculation French, out of Pass Matriculation French book, rippling merrily around. As I was only just turned nineteen, the senior pupils were nearly as old as I was, one or two perhaps quite as old and one at least a good deal older. He was preparing for the ministry, and with my help he ultimately got there. The others in the senior class were preparing for Pass Matriculation into the University of Toronto, Arts, Science, or Medicine. Of these, my first pupils, local pride in Uxbridge still honours the memory of Colonel Sharpe who gave his life in the Great War.

The teaching of Matriculation French and German was easy to me because I had been trained in exactly that kind of stuff. In reality it belonged to that futile and worthless brand of teaching French in Ontario which has so long disfigured the otherwise high standard of the province. It was based purely and simply on the final goal of a worthless examination consisting of translating English into French and French into English. Observe the result. Pronunciation didn't matter. Whether I pronounced well or ill, and whether my class pronounced still worse or rather better, was of no consequence. There was no test in pronunciation, no requirement of reading out loud. Nor did it matter in the least whether they understood French when they heard it spoken. There was no test in dictation, no question and answer, nothing but written French—dead as a dead language. On the other hand, there was a regular egg dance of ingenuity in translating verbal phrases and such back and forward—things like "Give him some of it; do not give him any of it. Speak to me of them; do not speak to me of them," and so on, endlessly. Anybody who has ever learned to translate in this way will never be able to speak or use French. The English words crowd into his mind. What he does is to think in English and translate into French. In German things are not so bad. The two idioms, being so similar in translation, keep tending to merge into actual use of language, if one will let it do so.

The whole fault with Ontario French arises in the Provincial examination and floods back to the source from that, like water checked by a dam. Once introduce dictation as a test of comprehension and reading aloud as a test of pronunciation, and the whole thing would alter. As it is, Ontario French isn't in it with French learned out of a phrase book as best one can with pronunciation given by those who know it. In any case, language for use can be learned only word by word and phrase by phrase. We learn to say *carte blanche* by saying *carte blanche*; learning off a list of feminines won't help.

But there is my class waiting. I must get back to them.

My salary was seven hundred dollars a year and seemed a lot of money: $59.33 a month. In a way it was a lot of money. Board in Uxbridge in 1889 was twelve dollars a month, washing about two dollars. All the clothes I would need in a year would represent about one hundred dollars, or eight dollars a month, drinks (meaning, say, a couple of glasses of beer a day, at five cents a glass) about two dollars and a half a month, the bars being closed on Sunday. That was all the necessary expenses, and all the remaining money was extra. One hardly knew what to do with it. There were, of course, no moving pictures, no soda fountains, no motorcars, no paid dances, no slot machines, none of the hundred-and-one odd expenses that make the life of young people today one continuous expenditure of money big or little. I forgot tobacco in my list above: call it a plug of "T and B" once a month at twenty-five cents.

I felt so rich on receipt of my first salary that I hired a "livery rig" (charge one dollar for the trip), a cutter, and drove over to the old farm, one afternoon to go there and back the next. I have always hated the care of horses from my early recollections of chores on the farm, but of course I could, like anybody else, drive a horse if I had to. I remember that a wild blizzard came on that evening with big snowdrifts and that I turned into a farmhouse, half frozen, to thaw out, or to thaw the horse out, I forget which. When I got home I gave ten dollars of my salary to my mother, the first instalment of relief to her finance, seeming like the first relief of Lucknow. It proved to be only the first of plenty, for as the years went by my brothers and I were able to give her help, and then when two or three of us became well off we were able to banish all her money perplexities and give her everything she needed. The long evening of her life, for she lived to be ninety, paid her back dividends on her past devotion. The cottage beside the river which my sister Rosamond built for her use at Sutton remains, a marvel of beauty of site and scene which even the passing motor tourist pauses a moment to admire. My mother lived there in a network of perpetual correspondence and casual visits from children and grandchildren, her house a sort of family centre, a No. 10 Downing Street, reaching out across the continent. She was so habituated to being in debt that, manage as she would, Mother always carried a little cloud of debt along with her. But it made no difference. We wiped it off the slate every now and then and let it go at that. Perhaps, after all, there is more in raising a large family, in spite of all that it entails, than many young women of today are inclined to think.

I worked away contentedly enough at Uxbridge. But of course the situation carried with it the drawback that, as I reckoned it, I was getting nowhere. I had dropped out of college and saw no way to get back and finish the two years towards my degree. To try to save money to do so on my high-school salary would have taken years and years. To settle down and try to make my life and get married and live on a high-school salary was a thing I never thought of for a moment. I tried to do a little odd study at my college books but did not get very far, and in any case teaching every day from nine to four was sufficiently tiring to leave little energy for anything else. Teaching, like anything else, is immensely tiring to a novice; later on it gets less and less so in proportion to one's ability to teach. But it is never easy, except to people who can't teach at all or don't try to.

On such terms I finished out my first half year

at Uxbridge and went up to Lake Simcoe for those summer holidays beside the lake which have played such a large part in my life for over half a century. My mother had again rented the old parsonage, the ancient tumble-down habitation of the first parson of Georgina of which I spoke before. I had also a sailboat, acquired in Toronto a year or two before from a remnant of my mother's temporary affluence and my father's temporary gains of the Winnipeg boom. It was what was called a double lugger, but I put it into a higher class when I brought it to Lake Simcoe by getting a local farmer boatbuilder to convert it into a single-masted sloop. Operations of this sort, which sound as if they ought to cost a couple of hundred dollars, then represented only about five dollars plus the price of a little paint. That was the first of a series of sailboats of varying sizes and rigs which I sailed on Lake Simcoe and its sister lake, Couchiching, from those days until now.

The marvellous thing of the good old summertime of those days was how little it all cost. I remember some years ago, at my present country house in Orillia, a medical man, a contemporary of mine, explaining to a group of people how he and another medical student used always to take a six weeks' holiday of summer camping and that all it cost them was twenty-five dollars each. The up-to-date auditors could scarcely believe it, but my medical friend was easily able to prove and over-prove it. He and his fellow students owned between them a canoe and a tent and blankets. So there was their lodging for nothing. For food they had a certain amount of canned beef and canned salmon or sardines, which, along with fish that cost nothing but the easy catching, represented a meal bill of, say, ten cents a day each. For milk they went to farmhouses along the lake and got all they wanted at five cents a quart, and the farm people felt so mean at charging anything that they "threw in" a lot of vegetables; or they bought vegetables and the farm people felt so mean that they threw in the milk; and if the campers came back a second day the farm people threw it all in. So there was their board. For light they had a coal-oil lantern at twenty-five cents a month. As to drinks, it is astonishing how little young people (not old soaks) drank before the days of prohibition: an odd glass or two of beer, when in reach of a bar, at five cents a drink, and a bottle of rye whiskey at seventy-five cents a quart for first-class liquor, carried along in the canoe for a "snifter" in the evening. Calculated this way, one wonders how the two medical students could spend as much as twenty-five dollars each on their trip.

In the good old summertime of those days our chief diversions were boating, sailing, swimming, and above all lawn tennis, newly introduced and all the go. Swimming never took the form of mixed bathing except for a few "sissies" who might care for it. Girls in those days, when they went into the water, were equipped from top to toe with bathing caps, full bathing suits more voluminous than their ordinary dresses, and bathing stockings and bathing shoes. "Swimming" for them just meant getting wet with their clothes on. Ordinary young men of wholesome minds looked on girls in the water as a damn nuisance. But for tennis they came into their own, since we all played so indifferently and had so little idea of the smashing game that tennis could turn into that any girl who could stand up beside the net and prevent the ball from hitting her in the face did well enough for a partner. Here again was a cheap game. The grass court cost little trouble to make, no expert work, and people made it for themselves. The net cost three dollars and lasted forever, and the balls never got lost, since we hunted them till after dark rather than lose them. As yet no one had ever heard of golf, at least not in that part of Canada, except as a sort of crazy game played in Scotland by knocking a ball round among sand hills which forbid any other exercise.

But compare again the cost of our lawn tennis of the nineties and the cost of the golf of forty years later which drove it out. Golf meant a high cost to make the premises and build a clubhouse and fence, high annual dues; with that, suburban fares, green fees, caddy fees, tips, at least one meal at the clubhouse on account of the distance from home. In the prewar days I knew of many people in Montreal who found that they had all that they could do to keep up their annual golf subscription without attempting to go out to the club and play. Yet in Scotland and in England, where golf links were clipped by grazing sheep, where the "clubhouse" was just such a small building as might serve to drink Scotch whiskey in or smoke a pipe in a rainstorm, golf was carried on for years and years at an annual subscription, in ordinary country places, of five dollars (one guinea) a year. Many people have told me of cases of minor revolution when the subscription was moved up to two guineas. But very likely, for all I know, the game may have been overswamped by wealth and by the pretense of being rich that has swamped out for us in America so much of the inexpensive amusement of the past.

The good old summertime of 1889 being ended, I went back with deep regret to my teaching job, with no particular prospect in front of me. And then unexpectedly things began to open up indeed and in less than a month altered my whole outlook. It is possible that the market for teachers had taken a favourable turn, or it is possible that I had made a hit as a teacher and that this one or that one may have spoken of me to someone else, but at any rate, quite unexpectedly and unsolicited, I got an offer to come to Napanee High School at a salary of nine hundred dollars—an increase of two hundred dollars in pay. By all the ethics of the teaching profession the Uxbridge trustees should have let me go or raised my salary. It is among the few redeeming points of the teaching profession that a school is not supposed to stand in a teacher's way: what is a temporary inconvenience to the school may mean a life advancement for the teachers.

The Uxbridge trustees didn't see it that way: they proposed to hold me to my contract. Looking back on it as I see it now, they felt that they had got a good article cheap and meant to hang onto it. They were, or most of them were, a poor lot. So they refused to let me go, and I had to accept it with the best grace I could and stick at my work.

Then right on the heels of this came a real offer, one that meant for me light out of darkness, salvation out of disaster. Upper Canada College needed a junior master at seven hundred dollars a year and offered me the job if I was free to take it at once. This would mean, of course, that I would go on with my college course towards a B.A. degree. For the residence requirements in those days were not strict, involved no actual roll call of attendance, and in any case, since the Upper Canada School day finished at three o'clock, I would take odd lectures that came at four or five. What it all meant to me I can find no words to describe.

But the Uxbridge trustees hardened their hearts, and again they refused to let me go. No doubt they were more than ever impressed with what a fine cheap bargain they had picked up. But this time the refusal was too bitter for me to sit down under it. I asked leave to come and talk to the trustees in person. They consented, and I went down to an evening's meeting of the board of trustees and laid my case before them with something, I imagine, like impassioned eloquence. I tried to show them how much it meant to my future. I took up no other aspect of it. I had no precedents to quote, no usage, no real argument, just how much it meant to me. It didn't seem to touch them. The chairman explained the difficulty of getting a new teacher when the term was already three weeks old, and that seemed likely to be the end of it, when to my surprise an elderly trustee who hadn't spoken—his name was Britton, and I am glad to honour it—hit the board table with his fist and said, "Damn it, gentlemen"—or words to that effect—"let that boy go. Do you think you can keep a boy of his ability in a place like Uxbridge?" With that the situation was saved: on a sudden inspiration I asked them to give me a week to find them a teacher and they consented.

The situation, I say, was saved. For it so happened that "my remarkable uncle," E. P. Leacock, was on one of those visits from the West to the East by which he eluded his creditors in the West, and I was able to enlist his services on my behalf. I have written elsewhere of "my remarkable uncle" and of the phenomenal career that made him one of the notable figures of the spacious days of the Winnipeg boom. He amassed a great fortune, on paper, went up like a rocket, and came down not like a stick, but with the more varied and graceful descent of a parachute. I wrote to him in Toronto, and he set to work at once with characteristic energy, interviewed the principal of Upper Canada and obtained a few days' delay, and in those days, with the aid of the teachers' lists and a flood of telegrams (there were as yet no general telephones), he unearthed a teacher, a modern-language teacher. It is true that his candidate, when produced, looked far from modern and short on language; indeed, I believe the good old man was hauled out of retirement, but he filled the bill and I was free.